# Shakespeare and the Common Man

GRAHAM WILSON

# Shakespeare and the Common Man

Millrace

First published in Great Britain in 2001 by
Millrace
2a Leafield Road, Disley
Cheshire SK12 2JF



ISBN 1 902173 10 4 (HB)
ISBN 1 902173 11 2 (PB)

Typeset in Baskerville BE Regular.
Printed and bound in Great Britain by
Bookcraft (Bath) Ltd, Midsomer Norton, Avon

# Acknowledgements

If you write a book about Shakespeare, you quickly realise the difficulty of acknowledgement. So much has already been written that inevitably you have assimilated the ideas of others which later you parade as your own. As it is, it would be difficult to recall and tedious to list each possible influence.

However, I must particularly acknowledge Martin Banham's '*The Merchant of Venice* and the Implicit Stage Direction', Andrew Gurr's *William Shakespeare*, Barbara Heliodora C de Mendonça's '*Othello:* A Tragedy Built on a Comic Structure' and Richard Dutton's *William Shakespeare*. These works specifically set into being trains of thought that formed the basis of various chapters within the book.

I hope those who might, quite reasonably, feel that they have been overlooked are sufficiently generous to regard their inclusion as applause rather than larceny on a grand scale.

I would also like to thank Faber & Faber for kind

permission to include an extract from Tom Stoppard's play, *The Real Inspector Hound.*

Graham Wilson
February 2001

# Contents

# The Reluctant Anarchist

It must have been at the time when my interest in Arthur Ransome had begun to wane and I had yet to discover Leslie Charteris. It was then that I remember thinking I should read Shakespeare. I wasn't sure what Shakespeare was, but I knew it was important because when my mother mentioned his name, she used that tone of voice that she normally reserved for the King. I assumed therefore that Shakespeare was to writing what Len Shackleton was to football or Denis Compton to cricket.* Of course, today's youth is under no such cloud of uncertainty. Benevolent educationalists (conveniently ignoring their own memories) force-feed the young with a diet of literary worthiness, knowledge of which they test at appropriate intervals with such socially aware

* *Bowing to my publisher's opinion that the above literary and sporting luminaries are somewhat antediluvian, I proffer the more volatile substitution of (a) J K Rowling, Stephen King, (b) David Beckham and Shane Warne.*

probings as: *Oliver Twist! Is he (a) a scrounger? (b) a reconstructed Marxist? or (c) a future Lord Mayor of London?* In the world of the tick-box, Dickens is big but Shakespeare is better. Whatever the dietary whim, Shakespeare is the staple.

So today's child who can now lisp his or her way through the canon from *Titus Andronicus* to *Timon of Athens* would have mocked at my dithering as to which play I should read. As far as s/he is concerned, what is to be read is what has been prescribed and what has been prescribed is to be read. Anyway, I settled on *Macbeth.* A glance at a cast list of Witches, Bleeding Captains and Assorted Murderers sounded promising, as did the virtual absence of names ending in *o.* I have to say I was disappointed. Even my most determined patriotism could not persuade me that the scenes of the supernatural were a match for Edgar Allan Poe. The murder of Banquo (I should have heeded my reservation about Italians) was a quick *Look out behind you!* and *Oh, I am slain!* and as for the denouement, The Shootout at Dunsinane Creek would have been jeered off the screen at any Saturday morning children's matinée. There *were* one or two memorable lines. 'What you egg! Young fry of treachery!' springs to mind but for the most part the story seemed to be about people talking to themselves. It was then that I remembered that my mother also adopted the same hushed tone when talking about those unfortunates who 'weren't quite right'.

Fortunately and, as I was to discover, typically, the Saint arrived in the nick of time and, returning the *Complete Works* to the dusty tramlines of my father's bookcase, I set about my examination of the Life and Times of Simon Templar.

It wasn't until O Level loomed that I again came across the dramatist. *Henry V*, the one and only part, was the prescribed text. The master who was responsible for the choice, if choice there was, took all the main parts in different voices and reduced any budding thespians to roles of minor impotence. In my case, the Boy. These we had to learn by heart to ensure that nothing interfered with the fluency and dramatic continuity of the main exposition. As the years went by, I realised that my dismissal of the Boy might turn out to be a little hasty. At the time, I thought no more about it except to admit that the alternative text, Scott's *Guy Mannering*, was a good deal more turgid and, once I discovered that the considerate

Mr Brodie gave the general detail more succinctly than Sir Walter, not really worth reading in its entirety. Thought no more about it, that is, until in a last-ditch attempt to place some semblance of the plot into the minds of the inattentive, the whole year was dragooned into the School Hall to watch the 1944 Olivier version on the flickering screen. The pleasure of missing Double Français with the redoubtable Madame G was intensified by the swish of arrows that mowed down the 'proud' and 'over-lusty' French. (I was disappointed to discover in later life that this apparently authentic sound effect, despite the best efforts of those London toxophilites too decrepit for active service, was eventually produced by twanging elastic bands.) I was also a little confused as the film did not seem an exact reproduction of the play, but there is more to life at sixteen than literary introspection and I didn't let it trouble me.

So Shakespeare and I parted company. Despite a wish or at least an inclination to study English in the Sixth Form, I was easily put off by the Senior Classics Master telling me that the Proper Study of Mankind was Plato, or disciples, and that English was really only suitable for women and other such second-rate minds. (At this stage, I had probably never heard of and certainly didn't understand the term 'vested interest'.) It wasn't until I started teaching English armed with little more than a Classical Education in tatters and a degree in law that I realised the flimsiness of my credentials, a fact reinforced by the slightly concerned queries at interview: *Do you feel sure you can manage examination classes in Literature as well as Language?* I must have impressed by my confidence, poised as it was on the first half of *Guy Mannering* and an eclectic selection of the American novel, and so I once more bumped into or, rather, made unavoidable contact with the Bard. After all, if you have to teach it, you may find it best to read it first. So read it and teach it I did–*Macbeth*, *Twelfth Night*, *The Merchant of Venice*, *Henry IV Pt 1* and, of course, good old *Henry Five.*

Although I was not surprised, I found it difficult to accept that my charges were less than enthusiastic. So I gave some thought as to why this might be. There is no doubt that teaching a text so that students can develop a formulaic approach to the Compare and Contrast type of question is unlikely to excite the enquiring mind but, eventually, I realised that there was more to it than that. If taught in the then accepted manner of Good Overcoming Evil and the Perils of Failing to Obey Authority, the words of Shakespeare merely echoed those they heard at Assembly every morning–words, in the liturgical portion, that even echoed the sound. Shakespeare was the Headmaster and the Headmaster was Shakespeare. Both had to be attended to in the interests of self-preservation but only endured in the safe knowledge that they would one day disappear. So I changed my tack, developed questions on the lines of: *Well, how would* you *like Henry IV as a father?* or *Macbeth! More mug than murderer?* and tried to persuade them that Shakespeare, far from being the pompous voice of Authority, was in fact on their side and that the plays, if given a chance, showed evidence of dissent and rebellion against the apparently approved conformity. What is more, viewed from a certain angle, they even cast doubts on the validity of the very arguments they seem to promote–the innate superiority of the European over the savage, the worth of Banquo as against the evil of the Macbeths, Henry V as a national hero, Hamlet as a noble mind.

How does this happen? A useful starting point is

the concluding sentiment of Edgar at the end of *King Lear*, Shakespeare's cataclysmic and, in its wreckage, most revealing play:

'Speak what we feel, not what we ought to say.'

At a glance, the play seems to follow the pattern or, rather, concoct a mixture of earlier political dramas. Machiavellian upstarts attempt to overthrow the existing order which has been weakened by the ill-advised actions of the monarch, fall out amongst themselves and are eventually squashed by a much put-upon figure of good. At this point, a Henry IV or vanquisher of Macbeth would explain that it was inevitable that good would inevitably prevail, along the lines of 'Thus ever did rebellion find rebuke,' etc. But with Edgar the response is different. Rather than a smug acceptance that his virtue had been properly rewarded by being offered a top job in Albion plc, he seems more concerned with the lessons to be learnt from the terrible events that dominated *King Lear*. Edgar realises that the society of which he has been part was founded on mental dishonesty and self-deceit. Under this umbrella of hypocrisy, evil had flourished until it had grown too powerful to be checked. It was only by starting again and abandoning any preconceptions about kingship and the nature of rule that any progress might be made.

So, it is quite possible that Shakespeare wished to take the side of the Common Man and attack the abusers of power and privilege and the sacred cows they invent to protect their position. But, in a world of the rack and the 'servant fee'd', it was clearly dangerous to say what you feel and equally politically advantageous to say what was expected. If the playwright wants to tell the truth as he sees it, this restriction places him in a difficult position. Shakespeare overcame the dilemma by appearing to say what he ought but, by applying a variety of strategies, allowing the audience to see what he felt and meant. The voices he employs for this purpose are, more often than not, ill-considered characters–rogues, fools, clowns, peasants, powerless women and, in one case at least, a boy. Once heard, they tempt us to look again at the true nature of, say, the ethnic outcast or the dysfunctional prince–to examine the way the playwright can place contradictory truths side by side and by this means raise equivocation to a high art.

# Better A Witty Fool

Of all the characters that Shakespeare could employ to voice revolt, the Clown or Fool was the most obvious. Every acting company numbered one in its midst and, regardless of the play, the audience would expect an interlude or two when he would be let off the leash to amuse them with his wit and knock-about routines. Even a play as nasty as *Titus Andronicus,* with its scenes of rape, mutilation and cannibalism, finds room for the Clown to amuse with his malapropisms–until the Empress of Rome loses patience and he comes to a suitably sticky end. In real life, such a character (a descendant of the Court Jester or all-licensed fool) might give offence without falling foul of the powers that be, in particular the powers of censorship wielded by the Master of the Revels. All scripts had to be submitted to his scrutiny and anything that tended to treachery or sedition would be struck out. However, a clown might get away with remarks that, in the mouths of noblemen, would have resulted in the author being hauled off to the Tower.

Given that they were there and he had to employ them, Shakespeare set about weaving the clowns into the fabric of his plays. They appear as porters and gravediggers, *inter alia*, and their main function is to offer sardonic and oblique comment on the action that is played before them and the audience. In a sense, either wittingly or unwittingly, they act as chorus or commentator to these events. It is only in the later plays that they move centre stage, first as Feste in *Twelfth Night* and then, most memorably, as the Fool in *King Lear*.

Whatever strategy Shakespeare may have planned in his use of the clown, there were practical problems in his way. Hamlet's imprecation that 'those that play your clowns speak no more than is set down for them' suggests there must have been a tendency for such actors to ignore the text and play to their own gallery or, worse, manipulate the script to include their own material. Shakespeare may well have wanted his clowns to contribute to the 'necessary questions of the play' but there are signs that he felt that they could not be trusted to behave.

The Clown was no inconsequential member of the troupe. In the case of Shakespeare's company, the Chamberlain's Men, the Clown was a fellow shareholder, Will Kemp(e). He would have a say in the nature of the productions and would certainly have wanted an opportunity to play to his particular audience. Although the two co-operated for a number of years, it seemed an uneasy truce as in 1599 Kemp broke away, leaving the company to dance his way to Norwich in a profitable testimonial performance. It may have been this insistence on dancing that upset Shakespeare. It was customary to end the play's performance with a jig–a bawdy and somewhat tasteless song-and-dance routine which probably originated to keep the audience in the theatre while the hat was passed round. If Kemp insisted on this performance, regardless of what had gone before, it must have been galling for the playwright to see the pathos that he had carefully created at the end of such plays as *Romeo and Juliet* mangled by the Clown's antics.

It is probably no coincidence that the more serious plays were written after Kemp's departure. The arrival of Robert Armin from Lord Chandos' Men to take over the role of Clown not only encouraged Shakespeare to rewrite some of the earlier parts to suit the newcomer but also allowed him, at last, to put into practice his more ambitious plan. What is certain is that the change of clown and the building of the Globe heralded the more perplexing comedies and the series of renowned tragedies.

But, up to that point, he had to make do with Kemp and it is a mark of Shakespeare's ingenuity that he was able to make a virtue out of this particular necessity. The part of the clown, Launcelot Gobbo, in *The Merchant of Venice* is a good example of how a compromise was reached. His essential part in the play is, as Shylock's servant, to aid his employer's daughter to rob her father and with the ill-gotten dowry run away and marry Lorenzo. As a reward Launcelot is freed from his tyrannical master and taken into service by Bassanio. However, the clown has two other scenes which are for the most part irrelevant in a present-day production.

The first opens with Launcelot's self-catechism. Playing the parts of his conscience and the devil, he debates whether he should or should not run away from the cruel Jew. Having decided he should, he bumps into his blind father who is seeking directions to Shylock's house. The directions are delivered too quickly for comprehension and, to add further confusion, Launcelot informs Old Gobbo that his son is dead. When tired of that joke, he admits that he is he and in fact alive and seeks his father's blessing. To achieve this, he kneels before his father, but about-face so that his father mistakes the hair on the back of his head for his beard. All very amusing if you accept the feeble and handicapped to be a suitable butt for humour. The knockabout farce might have been a concession to his Clown, but Shakespeare has given more to the part than that. The question as to whether you should continue to serve a cruel master is a microcosm of the larger debate as to whether you owed unquestioning loyalty to a bad king. A debate which, with the childless Elizabeth coming to the end of her life, could well have a bearing on all those listening to the play. Moreover, Launcelot leaving Shylock for Bassanio presages the greater escape and financial requital that Portia will arrange for Antonio.

The second scene occurs late in the play when Launcelot appears, with much caterwauling, as a superfluous messenger (Shakespeare has already arranged trumpets to that effect), announcing the arrival of Bassanio at Belmont. The point of the joke is that although the action is taking place in broad daylight, Launcelot is supposed to be delivering his message to Lorenzo in the dark. Ten references to the fact that it is night time make sure that the audience gets the point before the clown enters. This setting would give Kemp every opportunity to act the fool, bumping into pillars, tripping over imaginary objects, teetering on the edge of the stage and mistaking some stage prop for Lorenzo. Indeed, the actor playing Lorenzo might have been cajoled into playing his part as they bump into each other in the 'dark', etc. As Kemp has the last line, 'My master will be here ere morning,' he can spin the scene out for as long as he thinks the joke is worth. Thus, the 'necessary question' of the courtroom drama can passed unscathed and Kemp has had his moment. So both are happy.

These two scenes give ample scope for the twin weapons of a certain type of comedian–the humour that can be milked out of cruelty and catastrophe. But after 1599 Shakespeare no longer felt obliged to go to these lengths and could at last hope that his serious intentions would not be deflected by improvised and irrelevant remarks designed to amuse 'some quantity of barren spectators'. The play that was being worked on at this point of change was most probably *Julius Caesar,* which contains two minor characters–the Cobbler and the Poet. Both of these parts could have been written to be played by the Clown. However, they are two different sorts of clown and it would be admirably convenient to my argument if Shakespeare wrote them with respectively Armin and Kemp in mind. At the time of conception he might not have known for sure who would be playing what; it is even possible that the two clowns overlapped. The fact that contemporary evidence shows that Brutus' suicide is followed by a jig suggests that Kemp's hand was not far away.

*Julius Caesar* begins with the mob who have unilaterally declared a holiday to celebrate Caesar's victory over the sons of Pompey. The forces of law and order in the shape of the tribunes, Flavius and Marullus, are trying to get them back to work before matters get out of hand. But the cobbler, as the spokeman for his fellow workers, is linguistically far too clever for them and his equivocating defence gives him the edge over the pedestrian Marullus. What is more pleasing to a section of the audience is that he is able to hide this impertinence behind a quick-fire wit. Although it is still in the clownish tradition of the country bumpkin outwitting the sophisticated townsman, it now has a sharper edge. The target is more impressive and a portion of the audience would relish the sight of the common man putting one over his so-called betters. Although the cobbler's scene might appear at first sight to be little more than a comic aside, it soon becomes clear as the play develops that the mood of the mob and its attitude to the establishment have a crucial bearing on the outcome of events. Shakespeare will vary this role with the Scottish Porter and the Danish Gravedigger, both of whom not only are more than a match for their superiors but also make telling contributions to the central concerns of the plays in question.

The contrast with the second 'clown', the Poet, is clear. There is no serious comment. Rather, it is an irrelevant set piece which, like the part of Gobbo in the final scene of *The Merchant of Venice*, gives the actor the opportunity to play the fool to his own particular gallery. The apparent function of the scene is to give the Poet the chance to reconcile the quarrelsome conspirators, a scene which is again dramatically unnecessary as the audience already knows that Brutus and Cassius have made their peace. The plea is in the form of a rehashed version of Homer:

> 'Love, and be friends, as two such men should be;
> For I have seen more years, I'm sure, than ye.'

No doubt, the actor would emphasise the doggerel and with extravagant gesture do his best to send up the pretensions of the philosopher–poet that Shakespeare and some of his contemporaries were accused of adopting. Whether it was Kemp or not, the clown would hope to spin out the joke in his own time, but in this case another has the last word. Brutus rounds on him and imperiously dismisses the Poet as one of 'these jigging fools' who does not know his time. If this was a theatrical reprise of Shakespeare's opinion of his fellow shareholder, it must have carried an extra meaning for the contemporary audience and, indeed, been poignantly reminiscent of the recently staged dismissal of another great favourite, Falstaff, by the newly empowered Henry V.

What is certain, however, is that the role of the Fool/Clown takes on a different hue at the turn of the century. An early appearance was in the comedy *Twelfth Night.* The play opens with the Lady Olivia entering into apparent perpetual mourning for the death of her brother and Malvolio, her steward, taking advantage of her lassitude to assume the role of master of the house. Feste, the Clown, acts as a commentator on their behaviour, exposing their respective affected self-pity and self-regarding pomposity. He shows that those with a high regard for themselves, who treat the Fool with little more than condescension or contempt, are, in reality, themselves foolish and self-indulgent. It is, as he says, a case of 'better a witty fool than a foolish wit'. Feste's astute observations on the weaknesses in human nature can seem little more than lightweight satire, but Shakespeare is only beginning and what appears relatively inconsequential in a comedy evolves into anything but a laughing matter in the tragedy of *King Lear.* But for the moment Feste, and perhaps his creator, are uncertain of the real nature of the part the fool has to play. As Feste explains in the song that brings the Christmas indulgence to its close, if the matter is trivial the fool's comments will be indulged, in the manner of mischievous pranks performed by small boys. But if it were serious, the world would bar its door against him and brand him a thief and knave. His conclusion at this stage is to abandon the unequal struggle and drown his sorrows–a somewhat different envoi from the jigs and 'bawdy chaunts' of his predecessor.

A couple of years later we see in *Timon of Athens* a small experiment that will lead to the greater role of the Fool in *King Lear*. Timon, in order to impress his friends, entertains them lavishly and beyond his means. He fails to heed the warnings of his faithful steward or the more caustic advice of a churlish philosopher, Apemantus. The latter is joined by the Clown in a scene where they confront the servants of Timon's creditors who, to while away the time, make the pair the butt of their jokes. Like Feste, the Clown proves that his tormentors rather than he are the truly foolish and, like his successor in *King Lear*, he sees truths that others see too late.

In the later play Lear, King of Britain, has decided, in an act of intemperate folly, to divide his kingdom between his three daughters. The two eldest fall in with this act of self-indulgence but the youngest,

Cordelia, refuses to compromise her honesty. She will not pay lip service to the flattery that her father demands. Lear, in a fit of pique, banishes her, dowerless, and when his faithful subject, Kent, intervenes, he banishes him also. With these two voices of reason out of the way, the self-seeking Goneril and Regan have a free field to dump their father and run the country as they think fit. So only the Fool remains to show Lear the error of his ways.

But the Fool that had emerged from Feste's chrysalis was made of stronger stuff than his progenitor and his attacks on Lear's aberrations in banishing his allies and empowering his enemies are more forthright. Not only, as Feste with Olivia, does he prove his master the real fool but he also shows that Lear's self-indulgent behaviour will lead to mayhem on a grand scale. By now, the Fool has been made into a central rather than a peripheral part of the drama. First, he controls key scenes at the start of the play. In Act I (iv) he has a series of speeches where he makes clear the extent of Lear's political and domestic folly. They mockingly echo the language that the king has used when addressing Cordelia on what he sees as her filial failings. The three 'nothings' followed by 'nothing will come of nothing' in the exchange between Lear and his daughter are repeated in this later scene. The Fool's song warning against self-indulgence is meant to be a lesson to Lear, a lesson that must be learnt before it is too late, another ironic echo of the warning to Cordelia to mend her speech 'lest it mar her fortunes'.

He is, moreover, entrusted with an important cornerstone in the fourhander on the Heath. A quartet which contained, in addition to himself, a fugitive acting the madman, a nobleman acting the peasant and a madman acting the King. The bewilderment that these scenes induce in the audience is channelled through a sane but similarly bewildered Fool. For the piece to work as tragedy and not slip over the border into farce requires enormous histrionic control from all concerned. Certainly not the place for your average jigmaker.

Some productions seek to reinforce the connection between Cordelia and the Fool by having the same actor play both parts. This would not be possible if the Fool was, as I have suggested, present at Cordelia's humiliation. They are two sides of the same coin rather than identical twins and the Fool's bitter tirade against Lear's stupidity and blindness gains extra weight if the audience has observed the Fool watching a fool set about his 'darker purpose'.

The coin in question is a composite of Shakespeare's Common Man, showing in turn scornful critic and compassionate realist. With this Fool, Shakespeare completes the transition from clown to an all-seeing Tiresias, a figure that powerlessly presides over the wasteland that unfolds before him.

It is easy to see why there is a desire to link Cordelia with such a figure. There is not only Lear's description of his murdered daughter as 'my poor fool' but also the genuine concern each have for the king's welfare. Both see the probable outcome from the very beginning, even if Cordelia is unwilling to explain her fears. Both possess the clarity of thought that might have resolved the situation but neither has the power to implement it. By the time Lear sees the truth of the Fool's assertions and Cordelia enlists the help of her husband (ironically, the King of France), Lear is mad and beyond redemption. If the link does exist, it might be interesting to see if any other of Shakespeare's women play the fool and if so to what effect.

# Neither Fish Nor Flesh

*Falstaff:* Setting thy womanhood aside, thou art a beast to say otherwise.
*Hostess:* Say, what beast, thou knave, thou?
*Falstaff:* What beast? Why an otter.
*Prince:* An otter, Sir John? Why an otter?
*Falstaff:* Why? She's neither fish nor flesh, a man knows not where to have her.

(*Henry IV Pt 1*)

Falstaff's jibe that the Hostess of the Boar's Head Tavern is a beast that defies zoological categorisation is more than his usual smokescreen to deflect attention from the non-payment of the bill. Both the player and his Elizabethan audience are aware that he is speaking no more than the truth. The actor taking the part of Mistress Quickly would be male and the treatment of the part was therefore open to a variety of theatrical ambiguity which probably precluded the projection of a genuine female 'voice'. The simple solution for the contemporary playwright when characterising women was to produce a stereotype that could be performed for comic or pathetic effect. The question is, does Shakespeare go further than this? Does he use his women, as he does his fools, to provide a comment on the affairs controlled by men?

In the earlier political plays women are, for the most part, marginalised, although such views as they are allowed to express do seem to throw light on the true nature of the dominant and usually domineering male. Shakespeare's later historical tetralogy, *Richard II–Henry V*, which traces the fall of the over-confident Richard and the rise of the more machiavellian House of Lancaster, gives a reasonable range of female characters who could provide him with the chance to develop their role beyond that of a mere cipher of complaint. Whether he does so is open to question.

In the first play, the Duchess of Gloucester is vociferous in imploring her brother-in-law Gaunt to reveal the truth and avenge her husband's murder. Though sympathetic, Gaunt refuses on the grounds that he cannot exact justice against the perpetrator, who is in fact the king. He is caught between his chivalric duty to help the kinswoman in distress and the need for unswerving allegiance to God's anointed deputy. Previously he has closed his eyes to this rather awkward situation and when they are prised apart, his only recourse is to retreat into the nostalgic comfort zone of his 'scept'red isle' which is conveniently surrounded by a moat of wishful thinking. As this dilemma of divided loyalties and how to deal with the problem lies at the heart of the drama, the Duchess's plea should act as a prologue to the main action and prepare the audience for the contentious debate that is to come. However, instigated by a woman, it is rarely presented in this light and at times omitted altogether.

Things get no better in *Henry IV Pt 1*, which follows the usurpation of Richard's crown. Henry, the new king, is immediately faced by a consortium of rebels, spearheaded by Hotspur, who hope to overthrow him and divide the land between them. Lady Percy, concerned for her husband's safety and at his indifference towards her feelings, desperately wants to be included in the action and implores Hotspur to confide in her and tell her what is really happening. Far from having her concerns acknowledged, she is dismissed as being unable to keep a secret, which is particularly ironic as Hotspur has already let the cat out of the bag. As for love, she is told that she will have to wait until he thinks fit. The truth, probably, is that Hotspur, who sees life as a glorified game of conkers, does not wish any deflection in his pursuit of honour. To discuss his military ambitions with a woman who might have advised caution would no doubt demean the whole enterprise.

What is more, this middle ground of common sense will never be occupied. As the cycle progresses, sentiment is shed and hard-nosed pragmatism becomes the order of the day. When, in *Henry IV Pt 2*, Lady Percy asks Northumberland why he reneged on his promise to support her husband at the battle of Shrewsbury, her father-in-law's response to the question of his perfidy and Hotspur's death is to tell her not to cry over spilt milk. By the time the final play is reached and all has been sacrificed for success on the field of battle, women have been elbowed to the edge of the stage, obeying orders without question and reduced, in the case of Henry V's future queen, to speaking in comic broken English to amuse the chauvinistic rabble. Rather than considering the female voice, it is clear in the world of driven political ambition that when the going gets tough, the toughs really get going.

Not that all of Shakespeare's earlier plays have women in such a reduced state. In the comedies, their forces, marshalled behind the skilful repartee of Beatrice in *Much Ado*, more than hold their own. But, there again, these are comedies and we are left with the feeling that, once the pipers strike up, the ado is about nothing that significantly matters. And though the drama queens have their moments, Lady Macbeth is patronisingly dismissed once Macbeth feels that he has found his feet and Cleopatra, for all her masculine-approved skills of billiards and big game fishing, is found to pull the plug when it really counts. If compared with the final defiant fling of such tragic heroes as Hamlet, Macbeth or a surprisingly agile Lear, the deaths of the female equivalent appear relentlessly low key, either collapsing under an unsustainable burden or as the victims of their own treachery. It seems that even Shakespeare did not have sufficient confidence in his young male actors to entrust them with the really tragic moment.

All this raises the question as to why, apart from

cocking a snook at the Puritan objection to cross-dressing, women weren't allowed to play the part of women. It couldn't have been incompetence; the plays themselves confirm that they could run a tavern in Eastcheap or a not insubstantial part of North Africa. Nor did they seem to lack the histrionic art, as the common vice of Shakespeare's hell-hags is their ability to deceive, to act the part of the dutiful hostess or the loving daughter. No doubt the defenders of male dominance paraded the usual practical/economic/aesthetic reasons for their exclusion: problems with the travel arrangements/potential paternity suits/ *Well, we can't have Portia popping out of court to breastfeed the baby, can we?*

A more convincing point could be the vested interest of the company sharers that would encourage the need to train young male actors for the established major roles that they would eventually inherit. But one supposes what lay at the heart of the rejection of the nascent Judis Dench was that her kind was considered (by those in control) to be insufficiently educated to understand what was really going on and it would take the developed male mind to comprehend and effectively re-enact the place of women in the grand design of things.

Later literary observations on women as actors pick up the theme. In Austen's novel *Mansfield Park*, no sooner has the paternal benefactor Sir Thomas Bertram gone to inspect his business interests in the Caribbean than the *absolutely forbidden theatricals* take place, with the consequent sexual shenanigans. It seems to be the case that no sooner have the parents gone on holiday than the kids, with some help from their friends, trash the house or, in this case, the carefully constructed moral fabric. A second example comes from Forster's *A Passage to India.* Here, when indulging in Amateur Dramaticals at The Club, it is the women who close the shutters so that the locals cannot see the memsahibs acting out the emotions that they are so anxious to suppress in public. As the central episode of the novel is concerned with the *interference* with a European lady by an Indian doctor whose help she has enlisted to discover the true India, the established message is that you, if female, go native at your peril.

Both these examples would seem to support the idea that women had to be kept in check for their own good and allowing them freedom of expression or movement would inevitably end in disaster. But this impression is, as you would expect from such authors, at least partially misleading. In both cases men have initially laid down a series of conventions to control the behaviour of women. And conventions that are laid down under the pretence of protecting others usually have the function of advantaging the protector. Male activity at its most serious, Church, Law and Government, was and is an elaborate theatrical production with suitable costume and resonant expression. There is no doubt that letting women into a man's world would expose the myth of gravitas that it was at great pains to create and possibly women acting on the stage would have been the thin end of a rather larger wedge.

Of course, nowadays women strut the various stages of life. The sad thing is that if they, having broken down these fences, feel that equity has been achieved, they could be wrong. Now that there is a loss of interest in holding office, no longer any dignity in labour, and the work ethic bends to any half-baked entrepreneurial shortcut that comes along, men are more than delighted that women are willing to take over their former tasks. Tasks that, now open to scrutiny with its consequent accountability, are much too much like hard work. Much better to let the missus make the money and retire to the saloon bar to discuss the various strikers currently playing in the Premier Football League or the relative merits of the titanium-coated golf ball. *Do we hear the cry for equal pay? It's the very least the poor dears deserve!*

But in this male-induced gloom there is a chink of light. Viola, albeit a boy playing a girl in boy's clothing, is entrusted with the explanation of the real nature of the Fool and that puts her at least one step ahead of the menservants in *Timon of Athens* whose high-water mark of acumen is to realise that a fool is 'not altogether a fool'. At the beginning of the third act, Feste has left Viola on stage after a bout of verbal fencing which he has won on points. Although we suppose her assumed Cesario would have nursed his bruised ego in a less appreciative manner, her good nature is able to applaud the skill involved in being a fool:

> 'This fellow is wise enough to play the fool,
> And to do that well, craves a kind of wit:
> He must observe their mood on whom he jests,

> The quality of persons, and the time,
> And like the haggard, check at every feather
> That comes before his eye. This is a practice
> As full of labour as a wise man's art:
> For folly that he wisely shows is fit;
> But wise men, folly-fall'n, quite taint their wit.'

She, as a fellow refugee, is a more than suitable candidate to comment on the classic outsider, the all-seeing but powerless fool, and is quick to realise that foolery is a form of wit in the sense of intelligent observation. But this wit contains other elements. It is not only entertaining and light of touch but also evasive to the extent of cunning–the wit Viola has employed to secure her own safety. In addition, the Fool's method of self-preservation is given a more sinister turn by the reference to the 'haggard' or untrained hawk. It seems that the butts of his jokes are also his prey. To 'check at every feather' suggests that he would seek out each and every weakness in a relentless and sustained attack. Provided the fool's targets deserve this treatment, this is the proper function of satire; the deflating of Olivia or Malvolio is perfectly acceptable, as is the mild gulling of Viola. But what happens when the victims are innocent and the fool feeds on their innate weakness for his own, possibly sadistic, amusement? If Iago should turn out to be a hawk in fool's clothing, then Viola has indeed been given a point worth making.

Shakespeare, if he really wanted to raise women to the level of acute observer of the folly perpetrated by a male-dominated world, could have gone further. Boy plays girl offers a variety of theatrical opportunities ranging from the bawdy to the absurd. But boy plays girl plays boy offers a different level of sexual ambiguity. According to Viola's decision when first cast on the shores of Illyria, Shakespeare originally intended that she should disguise herself as an eunuch. Apart from the obvious advantage in avoiding any slip of character enactment when seeming to be a man, it would have provided the opportunity to allow the sexually androgynous Viola to act as a foil for the socially and politically androgynous Fool. In such circumstances she could really have *played* the fool in every sense of the word. In the event, Shakespeare changed his mind and had Viola apply to Orsino's court as a page, and the opportunity is sacrificed for the possibility of comic sword fights with jealous rivals and jokes about beards. He probably decided the nature of the drama did not warrant such a juxtaposition and chose to postpone the pathetic possibilities of the beached female and the omniscient fool for a more weighty occasion.

So, the question remains–have women been raised to the rank of fools? Perhaps Cordelia had some idea of the treatment meted out to her predecessors. If so, she could have not been confident that, even in a supportive role, she would have been given a reasonable hearing. No wonder she kept her mouth shut.

# Sorting The Men From The Boys

It is not only women who have to keep their mouth shut. In times of war, any views contrary to the general 'effort' are best kept to oneself. Any departure from orthodoxy is seen not as an exercise of the right to assert a personal opinion, but as a deliberate act to undermine all that our brave lads are fighting for. This was never so evident as during the attempt by the British Government to lord it over Argentina in the Falklands War or, as the more alarmist factions had it, *The Falklands Crisis.* No one seemed to promote a concerted attack against the venture on the grounds that it was not only perpetrated but also prolonged with the main purpose of saving the political careers of the two leading protagonists. What happened to the outcry that should have burst forth at the idea of a corrupt dictator sending ill-equipped conscripts from the sub-tropics of an out-of-the-way province to fight a fully professional army in the wastes of the Antarctic Circle? Where were the tabloid headlines demanding fair play and democratic accountability? Even if you defended the rights of the islanders to maintain their own sovereignty, was the best solution to yomp over every foreigner in sight? The cartoon in the Russian press had it about right–two bald men fighting over a comb. The truth is that these questions were not asked. In matters of political pornography the *Sun* rules, in this case ensnaring its readers not so much with the titillation of Page 3 as the excitement of vicariously rubbing Johnny Foreigner's nose in the mud or, on this occasion, permafrost. What seemed to be forgotten in the undignified scramble for Post Imperial Triumphalism is that war, like killing in self-defence, is under appropriate circumstances justifiable, but both deeds are still acts of homicide and, as such, a fundamental violation of human rights.

Yet, at the start of the First World War, Herbert Asquith, son of the Liberal Prime Minister, wrote a poem entitled 'The Volunteer'. It opens:

> 'Here lies a clerk who half his life had spent
> Toiling at ledgers in a city grey,
> Thinking that so his days would drift away

With no lance broken in life's tournament.'

and, after much recondite imagery involving gleaming eagles and oriflammes, it finishes:

'And falling thus he wants no recompense,
Who found his battle in the last resort;
Nor need he any hearse to bear him hence,
Who goes to join the men of Agincourt.'

Although the poet's family connections might lead the cynical to assume that this was an overt piece of political propaganda, it is possible that in 1914 the men on the Clapham omnibus weaned on the rectitude of the British Empire might have really believed that they were setting out to destroy the Anti-Christ. It took the combined efforts of war poets such as Sassoon and Owen to show that, whatever merits there were in dying for one's country, the concept of it being Dulce et Decorum was not one of them and in its aftermath the war was seen, by those prepared to look, for what it really was.

So, by 1944 no one could justifiably hide behind the idea that war was glorious, that the enemy could be defeated–as on the field of Agincourt–at little more cost than a token diminution of the ruling classes, a couple of dozen peasants and Davy Gam, Esq. Yet it was in this year that Olivier in his film production of Shakespeare's play *Henry V* set out to do just that. In case there were any doubts as to motive, the production was dedicated, in an opening credit, to the Commandos and Airborne Troops of Great Britain, which rolled over an appropriately solemn silence. As this was Shakespeare, only a fraction below the Bible in terms of Holy Writ, it would have been heresy to object to this commuted tribute to British heroism in the face of adversity. But was it Shakespeare or, to put it another way, was the message given the one the author intended?

It was only when I showed this, by now video, version to a group of fifteen year-olds and recognised a remembered relief that they no longer had to answer awkward questions but could pursue their preferred occupation of watching telly, that I recalled my early misgivings. As I now had a reasonable working knowledge of the text, it was clear that chunks had been omitted. This in itself is not necessarily devious for the film was, after all, a commercial venture and it made sense to cull lengthy expositions that were written in a language that a modern audience didn't speak and scarcely understood. What is worth considering is why the particular offending material had been cut.

When the shooting script was discussed, someone must have decided the film should show Henry's French Campaign as a just crusade, under no circumstances the product of imperialistic designs, and, what is more, the English hero king must be free from any taint of personal ambition or despicable behaviour. After all, the premise on which the previous four years had been based was to prevent precisely this state of affairs. The problem was that the play, at least, acknowledged these unfortunate possibilities. There is little doubt that Shakespeare expected his audience to remember the advice given to Prince Hal by his father–when the opinion polls are taking an alarming dip, it is best to 'busy giddy minds with foreign quarrels'–and realise that Henry was prepared to enter into a bargain with the Church to relinquish his pursuit of ecclesiastical revenues in return for its official blessing on his invasion of France. In the original, the Bishops of Ely and Canterbury go to considerable lengths to provide a watertight case to support Henry's probably dubious claims to the kingdom of France. In the film this is presented, as if live to an Elizabethan audience, as knockabout farce in which the intricacies of Salic law are reduced to little more than a much applauded slight against German women. The genuinely serious question as to whether Henry had any just rights in a campaign which was designed to save his political skin is therefore overlooked. As is the question of moral accountability that Williams poses to the disguised king immediately before the battle: *So what does happen to a soldier's soul if he commits mortal sins in a cause that turns out to be unjust?* Henry ducks the issue with a neat bit of sophistry, which shifts the blame from himself on to his soldiers by implying that they were probably going to hell in any event. The film just ducks the issue.

The portrayal of the Churchmen as feeble dodderers serves to point up Henry's sense of purpose and this is reinforced by the behaviour of the French king. In the film he is completely pusillanimous, even fainting at the thought of an English invasion. Not much of an adversary, you might think. However, there is a contemporary gloss to all this. Like the Vichy Government, he is too quick to bend the knee. Regardless of legal right, such weakness places on Henry, as it did on the Allies, the moral obligation to take over the country (or, in Stalin's case, countries) if only to restore the self-respect and secure the safety of its inhabitants. Without being specific, these scenes conjure up the image of the woolly liberal thinkers and paper-waving pacifists that stood in the way of a man determined to save his nation. If, on the way, such a man enhanced his reputation as the 'mirror of all Christian kings', the saviour of the many by the few, so be it.

The first cut of significance is a lengthy discussion between Henry and his advisers concerning the danger of a cowardly Scottish counter-invasion if they were to attack France. As the Commandos and Airborne Troops no doubt consisted of a number of Scottish soldiers, it would be understandably unfortunate to refer to their ancestors as 'weasels'. But the omission allowed the impression that all Britain was behind their leader, an untruth that surprisingly has a supporter in the original play. No sooner had it been decided that three-quarters of the army should stay at home than the Chorus, who is supposed to keep the audience informed, announces that 'all the youth of England are on fire' and the consequence of this conflagration is that England is only 'guarded with grandsires, babies and old women'. This in itself seems odd, but there are more serious omissions to examine. What other insights to the character of Shakespeare's Henry have been left on the cutting-room floor?

First, Henry's clever, if somewhat self-indulgent, humiliation of the English trustees waiting to seize power the moment the king's back is turned. Second, the warnings of (what might be described as gratuitous) violence in his response to the Dauphin, followed by the threats to the Governor of Harfleur that he will unleash his English troops in a wave of rape and murder if the town fails to surrender. (In both cases he places the blame for these potential atrocities on the victims rather than the perpetrators.) Third, the rather craven supplication to God to forgive him for his father's sins. And last and perhaps most pertinently, the flagrant disregard of whatever passed for the Geneva Convention, when he orders the murder of the French prisoners in an act of unnecessary revenge. In sum, on this evidence, a self-approving, superstitious violator of human rights. Again, a bit too near the contemporary mark for comfort.

Of course, it could be argued that a ruthless and egocentric streak is an essential attribute for any successful military leader and, as the end justifies the means, Shakespeare's audience would have found nothing exceptional in the portrayal of these qualities in their warlords. So why is the Olivier production so squeamish? Perhaps it was to distance itself from the comparison that Shakespeare was suggesting in his juxtaposition of Henry with the disreputable Pistol. The latter has a variety of scenes which, when placed next to those of Henry, might suggest that there is an artistic plan at work. These cameos are:

> *At Home:* Pistol arrives in Eastcheap with Mistress Quickly on his arm. An act of triumphalism, as he has scored a recent victory over his rival Nym. The marriage is clearly part of a more advantageous scheme, for with the Tavern come the dozen or fourteen gentlewomen that live by the prick

of their needles. He tries to mollify Nym with promises of the spoils of war:

> 'Let us to France; like horse-leeches my boys,
> To suck, to suck, the very blood to suck!'

*At the Front:* Like Falstaff before him, he is not over-enthusiastic about military commitment. He has enough swagger initially to impress Fluellen whom he patronises for his Welshness. At Harfleur he is quick to urge others to fill the breach and at Agincourt he is, in the heat of battle, conspicuous by his absence.

*The Victor:* Once any apparent danger has passed, Pistol finds a Frenchman more craven than himself and, with much verbal pyrotechnic, demands a ransom from his captive. Unable to speak French, he has to enlist the help of the humble Boy.

*The Vanquished:* Eventually his arrogance produces its own desert. He is forced to eat the Welsh leek that he has previously derided and given a good cudgelling for his pains. He also learns (despite some textual confusion) that his wife is dead and with her his Private Pension Plan. So, reduced to dining out on invented military exploits, he skulks off stage.

At first sight, the clearly deliberate placing of the Pistol scenes in sequential mimicry acts in Henry's favour–his bravery as against Pistol's cowardice, his modest behaviour against the other's arrogance. But it may run deeper than that. They are both flushed with early success–Henry in winning over the support of his previously sceptical subjects, Pistol in stealing Mistress Quickly from Nym–and both parade their new-won power. Their motives for the expedition to France are also uncomfortably similar. Both hope that domestic problems will be forgotten in the rush for the spoils, whether it be honour or loot. They both see that the scars of battle can be turned to their own advantage. Even at Harfleur, Pistol's expediency is eventually matched by Henry, neither wishing to jeopardise his particular long-term military ambition. What is finally interesting is to compare the 'French speaking' scenes involving Pistol with M le Fer and

Henry with the politically acquired French king's daughter. Both Englishmen have the upper hand and can afford to amuse themselves and the xenophobic audience by exploiting their superior position as they degrade the language of the defeated parties. Henry is less heavy-handed than Pistol but there is no mistaking the patronising tone.

And so, in the end, each Grand Design fails: Pistol's with the death of his cronies and Henry's, whose own untimely death reveals that the cracks of domestic unrest have only been papered over. In this respect there is a moment of unwitting support in Olivier's production. Before returning to England, Pistol is seen stealing a rather small pig, his solitary trophy, and scuttling off stage with it tucked under his arm. Shakespeare, of course, had no hand in this piece of dramaturgy. He was rather more subtle than that.

Moreover, there is another factor that almost overshadows any attempt to cast doubt on Henry's worthiness. This is the presence of an actor labelled Chorus who pops out at various points in the play to extol the virtues of the king and his brave band of brothers, to deprecate his Company's efforts to present such an egregious moment of history, to beat the drum and pluck the strings as the action demanded. So who was this sixteenth-century spin doctor and why did Shakespeare let him get his foot in the door?

His function would be familiar to the contemporary audience, used as they were to a weekly dose of being told what to think. And should be to us. For he is the figure of Squealer in *Animal Farm*, praising the efforts of his leader whilst explaining the need for the tightening of various belts. And, also, his clean-cut successor who was wheeled on to prime-time TV to explain, in a language that the ruling classes have honed to cut through any reasonable objection, *how our Brave Lads are faring in the South Atlantic Campaign.* And why it was necessary to restore civilisation as we know it, and, albeit reluctantly, ask for the necessary sacrifices to ensure that end.

Popular history has Shakespeare playing this part and the film version is more than happy to pay homage to that possibility and also to the idea that the voice of the Chorus is the voice of the author himself. But it seems unlikely that a playwright of any substance would portray his personal views in words that are at best full-blown and at worst untrue. In fact, the Chorus is not expressing his own views at all, rather those of the Eternal Boss who wishes to propagate the belief that, to decode another wartime hero, 'Never have so Many... owed so Much... to Me'. More likely, the author's plan was to give the character sufficient rope and there are times when his extravagance sounds at least one false note. Especially if you subscribe to the tenet that the louder he talked of his honour the faster we counted our spoons. However, if this was true you would expect another compensatory voice to present the more considered view.

And there is another commentator in all this: the Boy, dogsbody to the rabble of Eastcheap. Not that Olivier gives him even that much houseroom. Young as he is and the least important (if you exclude women and Frenchmen), the Boy is nevertheless allowed a number of observations. In his soliloquies we see the most sober analysis of the activities before us. He is not slow to realise that he is being exploited by his masters and that, regardless of his God-given duty, they have no right to expect him to commit crimes on their behalf. What is more, he sees that at a practical level these self-styled 'Yoke-fellows in arms' are complete underachievers and he, unlike less perceptive observers, is not surprised that Henry is quick to execute his previous acquaintances when it suits his purposes. Even the Chorus, repackaged as Epilogue, is forced to admit that affairs will not turn out quite as expected and we at this point realise that the Boy's observations might easily apply to more weighty matters than the doings of Pistol & Co. Like the Fools that are to follow, insight comes from an unexpected source and his pointless death is as pathetically ironic as any of their observations. Indeed, its modest stillness is almost too neat an example of the assertion that one of the first casualties of war is truth.

Does it matter how the Play is presented? Shakespeare has been interpreted to suit a variety of causes from Methodism to Marxism. It is probably as easy to portray *King Lear* as a case for Women's Lib as it is the opposite. However, war is a different matter. It has particular consequences that usually affect most those who control the situation least. So it has to be worrying that a man who has contributed as much as any other to an understanding of human affairs should be hawked about to shore up the notion that war is a good thing, especially when being waged by the English. I am not saying that all the subsequent deaths and mutilations that have been inflicted in support of political ambition should be placed at the door of this particular film. But, whereas the original author had gone to considerable lengths to provide an even-handed view, Olivier and his advisers might now have cause to reconsider their interpretation. Even if only the worst they spawned were the vitriolic obscenities that pass for support in the cause of the national football team.

# The Three Stooges

All top men need a stooge in their retinue. And women too. Like the glamorous socialite who so generously befriends her Plain Jane, there is a 'special relationship' between the two of them. There is a deal. An understanding that they will support each other, symbiotically tending to each other's needs. In our case, every King needs a Court Jester. Someone who can be given licence without posing a threat. Someone who can be enlisted to gather court gossip but be put back in the drawer when no longer needed. Many of Shakespeare's Fools accept this lot, unwilling as they are to precipitate action, merely content to paddle in their own self-pity. But what would happen if one or more of these cat's-paws decided to take matters into their own hands? If, with an agenda of their own, they conspired to exploit this arranged intimacy? Or as Moon, the incessant second string, expostulates in Stoppard's *The Real Inspector Hound*:

> 'I dream of champions chopped down by rabbit-punching sparring partners while the eternal bridesmaids turn and rape the bridegrooms over the sausage rolls.'

If all Fools aren't stooges, does that mean that all Stooges are fools? Shakespeare created two such in Sir John Falstaff, would-be confidant to the future Henry V, and honest Iago, trusted lieutenant of the Moor of Venice. Their very names suggest the difference in their nature. Hal's foil announces himself with resonant, full-blown confidence whereas Iago scarcely has to open his lips to mouth his name. This is a difference that would be all the more apparent if the historical possibility of Kemp playing the former and Armin the latter actually took place. As Falstaff, Kemp's skills could be given full range of comic possibilities and 'he could speak no more than was set down' for him whilst exploiting his larger purposes. Armin's Iago would observe the mood of him 'on whom he jests' and, having found the weakness, work upon it as the elements upon an empty house. First lifting a tile to allow the rain to seep and weaken, then, with ever increasing acts of violence, reducing the edifice to rubble. To effect this, Iago had to find a stooge or three himself. In a sense, the differing nature of the two actors as clowns leads directly to their difference as dramatic characters.

Now, Hal has a clear idea how he will use his stooge. By associating with Falstaff and his disreputable cronies, he hopes to confirm his own reputation as a wastrel or worse. When he inherits the throne and changes his ways, 'his reformation glittering o'er [his] faults/Shall show more goodly, and attract more eyes/Than that which hath no foil to set it off.' The prodigal son will be clasped to the bosom of his relieved subjects. Using this as a springboard, he will build a case for an unequivocal right to the throne, based not on his father, who had usurped the crown and murdered Richard II, the rightful king, but by casting himself in the role of his great grandfather, Edward III, whose reign was seen as golden, trouble-free at home and victorious abroad.

This required two strategies: to see off his rivals, personified by the much admired Hotspur, and to persuade others to support him in mounting a successful campaign against France. Falstaff is integral in both these aims. Hal hopes that his behaviour will lead his rivals to underestimate his courage and determination and the later public act of Falstaff's banishment will symbolically demonstrate his seriousness on taking on the role of king.

Falstaff (as indeed would have Kemp) has an agenda of his own. He hopes to cultivate Hal's friendship and, under the cover of such patronage, line his own pockets. He also hopes to incriminate Hal by involving him in his nefarious activities and so use the threat of exposure as a lever to achieve his own ends. This plan turns into a parody of friendship. Falstaff persuades Hal to join him and his fellow villains in a robbery, hoping that the intimacies of being comrades-in-arms would cement their relationship. When Hal neatly sidesteps this trap by robbing the robbers and returning the money, Falstaff has no alternative but to take the hazardous path of real military action and join Hal and the King in their fight against the rebels. To this end he accepts a command of footsoldiers which he is to present at the Battle of Shrewsbury. As he admits to Bardolph, he 'misused the King's press damnably', enlisting only those who would buy themselves out and replacing the spaces with thieves and vagrants who, with no visible means of support, would be only too glad to join up, so avoiding the unwanted attention of Authority.

Although Falstaff does his best, he still arrives when the battle is in progress and is attacked by a ferocious Scot who apparently kills him. Simultaneously on stage, Hal is busy disposing of the rebel leader, Hotspur. After a generous valedictory speech over his rival's corpse, Hal spies the body of the fallen Falstaff and, in lines reminiscent of Hamlet's rather dismissive epitaph on Yorick, promises to have him embalmed by and by. Hal has more important things to attend to and leaves the stage to the two mortal remains.

Whether the part was designed for Kemp or not, there is no doubt that the action that follows offers ample scope for comic business. Falstaff, working on the principle that 'the better part of valour is discretion', has saved his skin by feigning death and has heard all that Hal has said. His jack-in-the-box resurrection, accompanied by the petulantly indignant '*Em*balmed?' would set the tone. Once he has brushed himself down, taken a drink from the bottle of holstered sack and surveyed the scene for any further stravaiging Scots, he would inevitably stumble upon the dead Hotspur. Initial response: fear of another more retributive resurrection. Considered response: who could deny that a merely wounded Hotspur had not in fact recovered and that it was Sir John Falstaff rather than the Prince of Wales who had finally dispatched the rebel leader? After much toe-prodding and tentative finger-poking, Falstaff summons up enough courage to inflict another wound and with this proof drags him in triumph to claim his just reward. When confronted with this apparent apparition who unceremoniously dumps the corpse at his feet, Hal is too taken aback to contradict Falstaff's claim and for once is unable to untangle the gross lies. So, at half time, it appears that the score is one all.

In fact, Hal's net gain is rather more subtle. In addition to using Falstaff as his foil, he is able to learn for the years to come. There are two skills that the burgeoning dictator needs to acquire: the ability *(a)* to deal with political opponents ruthlessly when they least expect it and *(b)* to persuade people to act against their own interests in favour of his. The first can be achieved by letting his enemies think they are getting what they want, then pulling the carpet from under them (cf. Cambridge, Scroop & Grey). The second can be realised by turning the inevitably unpleasant outcome into an unexpected reward (viz. an invitation to join the Agincourt Club, Hon Patron HRH). It is also not a bad idea to have a fall-guy or two up your sleeve.

Falstaff fits the bill. Hal needs to keep him on board until the moment when his rejection will have the greatest dramatic impact. To that end he is prepared to suffer the fat rogue's insults and, after the attempted robbery, protect him from judicial inspection. Falstaff, buoyed by his military exploit at the Battle of Shrewsbury, is thus confident that at the old king's death, 'the laws of England [will be at his] commandment'.

The second skill is more difficult to rehearse. There's always a chance you might make an irremediable mistake or show your hand too early. Better, by far, to have some dummy to do the run before you. Such a moment occurs when, with Lord Westmoreland, Hal overtakes Falstaff and his 'food for powder' on their reluctant way to Shrewsbury. Here he is able to sharpen his own political education by observing the pragmatist at work. Apart from the usual trading of insults, Hal seems somewhat withdrawn and leaves his senior officer to direct the action and inspect the troops. It may have been at this juncture that he realised a couple of things. First, he could in due course turn to his advantage the comparison between the accepted and traditional indifference of the captain towards his troop and a king's compassionate enthusiasm for the well-being of his army. Second, that you must not confuse compassion with sentimentality and, when appropriate, you sacrifice the cannon fodder to preserve the sons of yeomen who can fight in a more substantial and self-sustaining cause.

The second half is much the same. Hal, having redeemed his reputation with those that matter (which includes setting up the Lord Chief Justice as a future stooge) and having sorted out the mechanics of his own form of kingship, is anxious to put theory into practice. He awaits the death of his father as much as Falstaff who is boasting, to all who will listen, of the power he will hold under the new dispensation. There is something equally distasteful in their scramble for the booty as the final whistle approaches. But when it arrives it's been an early bath for the stooge and the 'Glorious Reign of Henry V' has begun.

The relationship between Othello and Iago is more subtle yet, in a sense, more simple. On the surface, Othello is the master and Iago the servant but the venue and the players make for a different mix. Othello is an outsider unused to the ways of the sophisticated Venetians. His status in the city depends entirely on his military success rather than any claim to civil rights, as the ease of his arrest by Brabantio shows. He needs some way of discovering what is going on and someone to guide him through the maze. Honest Iago seems all too happy to meet these needs.

Unlike Hal, who makes a conscious choice to employ Falstaff for his own ends, Othello does not realise what Iago is planning. He takes him at face value, a trusted lieutenant that has his captain's interests at heart. In fact, Iago is really interested in manipulating others as part of his private game. By pretending to be their friend, he plays one off against the other, inventing imagined grievances and misinterpreting events to support his case. It may well be that he feels that he has been wronged by Othello and Cassio but this is not the genesis of his evil. The gulling of Roderigo, whose purse he had as if the owner, suggests a long and accomplished practice.

Iago's plan is simple: to destroy Othello and Cassio and despoil the innocent Desdemona. He hopes to arouse Othello's jealousy by hinting at an affair between Desdemona and Cassio and fire it to such a pitch that the Moor orders him to kill Cassio. Then, to persuade the lovelorn Roderigo that his only hope of winning Desdemona is by killing his rival Cassio. After this has been accomplished, to kill Roderigo himself in a citizen's arrest, thus removing any incriminating evidence. He can then count on Othello's jealousy and anger at being duped by the Venetians to be so uncontrolled that he will kill Desdemona, then be arrested and executed in turn.

So, what has to be done, once he has Othello in his pocket, is to turn Roderigo and Cassio into his stooges. The elaboration necessary to achieve this leads to his downfall. Cassio is only wounded and the need to involve his own wife, Emilia, in the deception over the incriminating handkerchief means that his contradictory lies can be discovered. Critics have been surprised that, when faced with his iniquities, Iago shows no remorse or indeed any other emotion. But Iago's ambition bears no resemblance to that of Falstaff. Whereas the latter was quick to brag about the control he had over the future king, Iago's pleasure lay in the fact that when his grand guignol was exposed to the horrified audience of Senators, only he would know what had really happened and that secret would remain for ever in the hands of the master puppeteer. He had never had any intention of saying anything.

If Hal had witnessed these affairs, he would have held them up as a justification for his ruthless behaviour, an unfortunate necessity if we are to control the Falstaffs of this world and nip the nascent Iagos in the bud. But possession of such a *carte blanche* will not prevent the unforeseen and motiveless act of evil and can be misused to remove anyone that stands in the holder's way. The idea that authoritative power is used for the common good does not bear close examination, but no doubt the good Senators of Venice would argue that by and large people got what they deserved, with the possible exception of a couple of women who found themselves in the wrong place at the wrong time.

All this is dreadful enough but the drama itself hints at an even darker side of human nature. In an earlier play set in Venice we again see the outsider destroyed by the ruling classes. When Shylock is outwitted by Portia, it seems to prove and approve the moral and intellectual superiority of the Venetians over the Jew and therefore, by implication, over non-Christians at large. *The Merchant of Venice* is a comedy and there is no doubt that the contemporary audience would feel that all was well that ended well. In the best seats (for the Court was at Windsor at the time), the merchant would be satisfied that his counterpart had come off the better but avoided breaking his word, and his lady wife delighted that Portia's father had sufficient foresight to frighten off drunken Germans and outwit the Prince of Morocco with his unwelcome hue, yet allow her to marry that nice Signor Bassanio. Even the groundlings would have been cheered that Jack-the-Lad Launcelot Gobbo had pulled the wool over the eyes of his tyrannical master and engineered the theft of Shylock's daughter and fortune. It would be a well satisfied party that wended its way back to the smug security of the city walls.

This is not to say that *Othello* is a comedy but there are some awkward echoes of the earlier play. Both Shylock's and Othello's possessions are confiscated to the benefit of sundry Venetians and this seems to be a main concern of the judicial proceedings. Not much evidence of God-given mercy in either case. The fact that the accused are strangers in the land counts for nothing. In fact, the maxim *Ignorantia legis non excusat* was specifically designed to keep outsiders in their place. In his final speech, Lodovico is quick to wash his hands of the whole affair and return to his Gentleman's Club in Venice. It would be interesting to speculate on the nature of the debriefing that he would have to make to the Duke. *After all, the threat of invasion had receded... a redundant Moor might have startled the horses... all very sad, of course, but quite convenient in a way.*

Indeed, the plot, with its misinterpretation of innocent action, dropped handkerchiefs and the eavesdropping Othello assuming a conversation about Bianca to be referring to his wife, could easily belong to the comic genre. In a sense, *Othello* is a distortion of the Italian *commedia.* Especially in Act One, there are strong parallels. Brabantio's behaviour is that of the traditional old fool Pantelon whose daughter marries against his wishes, much to the amusement of various disreputable lookers-on (again echoes of the merchant of that city). Iago is the Harlequin who appears to serve his master whilst trying to further his own ends, Desdemona the *amorosa*, Bianca the courtesan, and so on. Though there is little point in trying to lay the work of the *commedia dell'arte* as a template for *Othello*, there is more than enough to direct a first-time audience into the belief that they were about to witness a comedy. If this ran its normal course, Iago would score a few points but eventually his house of cards would collapse, the truth revealed and the malcontent suitably punished. The fact is that, unlike Falstaff, Iago is able to disguise his plan for a sufficient length of time for the damage to become irrevocable. With the two Venetian plays in mind, perhaps we should recast the definition of comedy: it is something that ends well for you and yours, regardless of the suffering of others.

So, in the end, why did Iago do it? The reason he gives is one of revenge for the lack of preferment and the seduction of his wife. Neither case seems convincing. Well-connected Cassio was always favourite for the job of second-in-command in front of someone from the ranks and it seems unlikely that Othello would be wasting his time with a middle-aged housewife when the glittering prize of Desdemona was within his grasp. It is more likely that the answer lies in the violence of Iago's sexual imagery–imagery that suggests a brutal lecher, and lechery, as he admits, produces 'foul thoughts'. Given that rape is fuelled by such a desire to hurt and humiliate, there appears to be a singularly unpleasant voyeuristic element in all that Iago does and it may be no more than that. But if there is a motive, it seems to be envy. Iago desiring but unable to attain 'this man's gift, and that man's scope' sets out to destroy that which he cannot get. He is the vandal who runs a coin through the paintwork of a Rolls Royce. The second form of solace for the envious is taking pleasure in the discomfort of others, the eagerly awaited fall from greatness. When Iago plans his strategy he has this 'double knavery' in mind and anticipates the outcome with obvious pleasure.

Three stooges? Hal certainly had one–and at least a couple in the pipeline. Iago, in turn, lined up a trio in Cassio, Roderigo and Emilia. But if any one was really stitched up, it was an innocent abroad who 'lov'd not wisely but too well'.

## What The Porter Saw

I have already expressed my early thoughts about *Macbeth* and later, if not necessarily wiser, reflection confirmed my suspicion that, though it is excellent in parts, there are one or two decidedly sticky moments. First is the speed with which Lady Macbeth persuades her husband to change his mind. Having convinced himself and the audience of the folly of killing Duncan, it takes no more than forty lines and a taunt or two concerning his manhood for him to cave in completely. I am not saying that, given time, Lady Macbeth could not have persuaded her husband to alter his opinion, but it is difficult to sympathise with a potential tragic hero if such a paragon of manly virtue jumps to attention every time the little woman snaps her fingers. It works better on film when the speeches can be interrupted by change of location, where space replaces time to give an impression of a considered debate. But Shakespeare cannot be blamed for the late arrival of Warner Bros and has to get his show on the road. There was no room for Pinteresque pauses or the interpolation of scenes where the unsuspecting victim is being pressed to yet another ironic scone by the attentive hostess while the nascent murderer broods up stage right. Nevertheless, the speed, as Hamlet remarked on the subject of baked meats, is difficult to swallow.

Act IV is of greater concern and seems to be the result of Shakespeare trying to write two different plays at the same time. The first and greater is of a man fired by ambition and an aspiring wife into an act of personal folly, the implications of which he only realises in the fullness of time. The tragedy is not that he fails in his enterprise, but that the nature of this particular success carries with it the seeds of inbuilt disaster. That the reality of his ambitious dream is no more than

'a tale
Told by an idiot, full of sound and fury,
Signifying nothing.'

The early scenes in Act V demonstrating Lady Macbeth's psychological collapse and Macbeth's desperate soul-searching bring this particular drama to its downbeat conclusion. The remainder of the act owes its existence to the second play, a mixture of the traditional history and the revenge genres. Evil thwarted by the forces of the good and the just, with a little help from their friends. And this is where the problems begin.

In Act IV the witches are no longer the shrewd, if mischievous, political analysts of Act I. Preceded by an unlikely Hecate, they in fact manipulate events to produce the required ending. Using the knowledge that Macduff was 'untimely ripp'd' and has left Scotland to support Malcolm in his attempt to recover the throne, they incite Macbeth (remembering the Banquo fiasco) to destroy Macduff's family, thus creating the necessary revenge figure, Then, with intimations of immortality, fuel the over-confidence which leads him to leave his castle whose supposed 'strength will laugh a seige to scorn'. The fidgety nature of Birnam Wood was presumably an inspired guess.

The murder in the second scene of Macduff's family is also curious as it appears to cast the play's redeemer in a rather poor light. Why leave his family at the mercy of Macbeth? Surely he could have taken them with him? However, the genocide is sufficiently atrocious to gloss over this question, not to mention the more uncomfortable query as to why one regicide can be more morally acceptable than another. If it is merely a matter of usurpation getting its comeuppance, then where does that leave everybody's favourite, Henry V?

The final scene is even more bewildering. Malcolm and Macduff appear to ad lib boring bits of Holinshed concerning the nature of kingship whilst waiting for Ross to remember his cue and kick-start Macduff on the road to revenge. If Malcolm does indeed suspect that Macduff is a double agent and is trying to test his loyalty, he seems far too easily convinced to the contrary and if his list of despotic extravagance is meant, by implication, to indict Macbeth, the shot misses the mark. Whatever other faults he may have, Macbeth has shown no sign of either licentiousness or avarice. The unwillingness of Ross to deliver his news and Macduff's reaction of surprise at what even he sees as highly probable, lack dramatic conviction. Small wonder that critics suspect another hand and wish to dissociate Shakespeare from any part of it. In fact, the whole act seems to exist so that the strings of denouement can be drawn neatly together with all the aplomb of a comedy. No doubt James I would be happy to support the idea that a new regime might mark a watershed where all previous evil disappears and a glittering future of hope and just prosperity is guaranteed. It may be that a seven year-old Oliver had other ideas on the subject.

So, despite its possible drawbacks as a play, examiners still prescribe, teachers try to teach and theatrical companies, inspired by crocodiles of earnest students, continue to perform. No doubt each was spurred on by the thought that even if the major staple of adolescent interest, sex, was by and large absent, violence, the close-run second, was abundantly provided for.

It has to be admitted that I was party to at least two of these follies. I not only chose the Scottish Play as the compulsory O Level Shakespeare, but pushed whatever luck there might have been left by unleashing my charges on a, fortunately not too local, amateur dramatic society. It must be assumed that the swelling of the company's coffers outweighed the inevitable eruption of sundry teenage philistines, once they realised that the escape from afternoon school did not compensate for two and a half hours of histrionic flatulence. It is not easy to describe the interaction between the audience and the performers but it made the response of the Glasgow Empire to English comedians appear positively sycophantic. I have no doubt that, under the cover of dark, Upper Five F added its share.

In fact, Upper Five F is probably a more interesting study of the human condition than the play itself. As the alphabetical suffix suggests, its members resided in the nether region of scholastic study, in matters academe more grave than grove. They fell into three groups: those fee-payers who had arrived so early into the junior part of the school that they could not easily be dislodged; those whom serendipity had favoured in the eleven plus; and the able but idle who, though destiny had initially placed them in the higher streams of educational excellence, had by this time successfully navigated their passage into calmer waters where they could indulge their ultra-mural enthusiasms in comparative peace.

Collectively, they were not the apple of the establishment's eye and, unlike the rest of the school that moved from classroom to classroom in the interests of extending the boundaries of knowledge, they were carefully concealed in the fastness of a building that would take a very large scale Ordnance Survey map to discover. Here, safe from the prying eyes of Her Majesty's Inspectors–or any over-curious parent–they were allowed to exist in a state of laissez-faire freedom that might have worried even the most ardent supporters of child-centred learning. Indeed, their very presence depended, in the main, on the ebb and flow of the scrap metal market. When the price is right, man profiteth more from irons in the fire than the conjugation of irregular Latin verbs.

To return. If Upper Five F was audience norm, it is little wonder that the performance was a complete disaster. Which, after all, is a theatrical triumph of its type. The young cannot escape blame with their varying suggestions of what Macbeth might be seeing before him and the inevitable pantomimic warnings on the appearance of Banquo's all too dramatical ghost. But the production did not help, with Birnam Wood masquerading as the leavings of a Wilmslow Garden Centre and accents that veered indiscriminately between Harry Lauder and South Manchester with the occasional glottal stop.

In fact, the whole affair was only salvaged by the appearance of the Porter. Not only did he wrench every possible ounce of humour out of his own speeches but he took full advantage of the fact that he had been given a number of bit parts, Messenger, Doctor's Bag-Carrier, etc. This required him to be on the stage or, at least, hovering in the wings for the remainder of the play. Realising that this was his fifteen minutes of fame, he decided to salvage the event single-handed. If he sensed that the audience was getting restless, he sidled downstage left and delivered a series of breathless asides to guide his charges through the more abstruse passages: *Malcolm, that's the bloke in the blue blouse, thinks the guy in the checked skirt might be one of Macbeth's side-kicks and he's sussing him out to see if he's kosher.* And: *A word of advice. Keep your eye on check skirt. He's on the verge of cancelling his widow-and-orphans pension plan.'* Alternatively, he would rework the more dubious bits of stage business from his earlier appearance.

There is no doubt that this produced pace and variety, the cornerstones of any successful dramatic production, though the thumbs-up to the witches as they dispatched Macbeth to his nemesis might be considered a tad indulgent. The remainder of the cast was torn between indignation at such Belittling of the Bard and relief at the thought that it was going to get home in one piece. Only the lighting man entered into the true spirit of the occasion, dimming the lights on the triumphant return of the forces of righteousness in such a way that it plunged the principals into stygian gloom and left a single spot illuminating the grimacing features of the true successor to Will Kemp. As one of the more discriminating members of Upper Five F, when asked his opinion on the events he had witnessed, put it: *Theatre, Sir, pure Theatre.*

In a more orthodox performance, the Porter is limited to the thirty odd lines at the start of Act II (ii), but that does not mean that the part is insignificant. Although Shakespeare needs the scene to allow the actors to scrub up and change into their night attire, he, as usual, makes more of it than that. The constant knocking hammers home the pointlessness of Macbeth's self-recrimination and the Porter, in his role of the Common Man, seems to see more of the truth than many of those around him. There may be an underlying point to the jokes of the stand-up comic.

The first part of the scene is a soliloquy. Hal has used the device as an aside to the audience to explain the reason for his strategy in consorting with rogues. Hamlet will use a number to reveal his feelings of moral and emotional uncertainty. Both take the audience with them. The watchers are invited on to the roller-coaster that will lead to the inevitable outcome. In the first case, to the glorious victory at Agincourt; in the second, to a morass of suicide and murder. With inside information, the watchers can anticipate events and appreciate each twist and turn. But the Porter has no such influence on events. So should we dismiss his bawdy comments and contemporary sniggering as no more than low relief?

Closer inspection suggests there might be more. The Porter's attitude is important. The verbal echo that mocks Macduff's demand for entry suggests a man who will open the door in his own time and will not scurry to every beck and call of his betters. Although only a minor act of rebellion, it implies he might have something to say about the greater treachery that has already taken place and the *You can knock as much as you like–it'll make no difference* attitude nudges into the memory the irony of Macbeth's just-heard wish that it would wake the murdered King.

The Porter's job is to tend the gate of Macbeth's castle, to allow entry to those who have a right, to deny admission to those who don't. This sets up the comic possibility where he can imagine that he is the Porter at Hell's Gate and so can amuse the audience by pretending to admit and then poke fun at figures whose discomforture would delight the groundlings. But the actuality is an ironic reversal. The Porter *is* a porter of hell. As soon as he opens the gate and admits Macduff, the struggle, in traditional terms, of good attempting to destroy evil will begin. Of course, the Porter is as unaware of this as he is apparently unaware that certain portions of Hell were frozen and that Dante's Ninth Circle of Hell was a below-zero torture chamber reserved especially for traitors. Yet even if the audience were equally ignorant of the intricacies of this particular Italian masterpiece, they certainly knew of the murder and suspected that the opening of the Gate could well reveal the treachery. So it is with a sense of curiosity that they await, in the interim, the Porter's choice of companions for the 'butcher and his fiend-like Queen'.

The man knew his audience and in the figures of the Farmer, the Jesuit and the Tailor, the Porter Clown is confident that he will be able to drum up the support of the ancestors of today's *Sun* readers. The Farmer's attempt to corner the market in grain and so force up the price of bread would have affected many and his getting his come-uppance would have had the ring of poetic justice. The belittling of the Equivocator not only pandered to the anti-Catholic phobia of the time, but it would also have been particularly pleasing that a smart alec, despite his clever arguments and manipulation of language, had been, in more senses than one, literally lost for words. The third perpetrator of sharp practice, the French Tailor, would also be a popular candidate for the drop. In a time when the customer provided the cloth, the Tailor would pretend that he required more than was necessary, then keep the remainder for his own purposes; a change of fashion seems to have revealed this particular fraud.

What the three have in common is that they fail through over-reaching, and thus prepare the audience for Macbeth's future over-confidence as a result of his visit to the equivocating witches. In particular, there is, and will continue to be, a parallel beween his acts and those of the damned tailor. Egged on by his wife, he desires more than his deserved reward–the thaneship of Cawdor–and manipulates the situation to get more than his quota–the Crown of Scotland–a gamble the pair took 'on th' expectation of plenty', a gamble which eventually results in their self-destruction. This assessment is supported by the tailoring/clothing imagery that threads the play with robes that are, at various moments, borrowed, flaunted and eventually purloined.

There is also a neat interaction with the main plot and the Porter's exposition on the effect of drink. Just as drink and lechery are intertwined in his mind, so now are ambition and murder in the minds of the audience. As the lecher suffering from venereal disease will have to sweat for it (a contemporary remedy), so the Macbeths will suffer a similar distress for a 'mind diseased' which will roast their goose as surely as the lecher's. Ambition, like drink, might provoke desire but it similarly seems to undermine performance.

Macduff's insistent knocking has thwarted the Porter's hope 'to let in some of all professions' but it would be interesting to know whom else he had in mind, who else in the play might be treading 'the primrose way to th' everlasting bonfire'. There is arguably a villain more despicable than Macbeth, someone who would be happy to see another doing the dirty work so that he can benefit in due course. Someone who might suggest a breathing space before instigating the investigation into Duncan's murder to give himself the opportunity to weigh up the situation before acting. Someone who, suspecting murder, does nothing about it, hoping that the murder might be to his potential advantage. Someone whose guilty conscience, even before the death of Duncan, prevented him from having a good night's sleep. In fact, historically, Holinshed has Banquo as an accomplice to Macbeth but, as he was an ancestor of the current king, James I, it would have been ill-advised for Shakespeare to pry too deeply into that role. Might this be the explanation for the limp Act IV? Could there have been a sub-plot hovering in Shakespeare's mind involving Banquo's double treachery to king and comrade-in-arms? Certainly the foundations seem to have been carefully laid. But this might have been a risk too many and the earlier hints are not pursued. Instead, he resolves the problem by having Banquo murdered and turned into a supernatural device. A device that so undermines the confidence of Macbeth that he is driven into the arms of the Weird Sisters and all the consequent folly. As neat a bit of equivocation as ever the Porter saw.

# All The King's Men

At the end of *Macbeth*, Malcolm is proclaimed king and rewards his loyal followers by making them Earls, so underlining what was then the general principle that the eternal struggle between good and evil was exclusively conducted between the noble good and the well-bred bad. The pattern was that blue-blooded evil pulverised the noble but puny good until they, or God, or both, decided enough was enough. They or He sent for a noble and particularly strapping good that the dramatist had thoughtfully kept kicking his heels in the wings, who then, to the relief of all, duly dispatched the bloody butchers and their fiend-like queens. The fact that the noble good probably had as little interest in human rights as his predecessor was shrouded by the fall of the final curtain.

But what happens when tyranny strikes and there is no available John Wayne to dash to the rescue? As *King Lear* poses such a problem, it is worth recapping the opening scenes. Lear has decided that he had done his share of shouldering the responsibility and chore of ruling Britain and has hit upon a plan to ease his way into early retirement. This was simply to divide his kingdom between his three daughters (and so, by definition, their husbands), then variously spend his time at their country retreats with a bunch of like-thinking chums, carousing into the small hours and chasing whatever form of prey took their fancy.

However, at this time Lear still had sufficient of his wits about him to realise that there was the odd loose end or two that needed tidying up. First, although Goneril and Regan were married to the Dukes of Albany and Cornwall respectively, his youngest and most favoured daughter, Cordelia, was still unattached. Second, he wanted to make sure that his daughters were properly appreciative of the gesture he was about to make.

He solves the first by lining up a choice of either the Duke of Burgundy or the King of France (equally useful for the all-year tan) and the second by extracting a public affirmation of the love that his daughters have for their father. To make the whole event more theatrical, he decides to turn this ritual of obedience into a competition to see which of the three can most impress with her filial affection. The reward for the winner was the rather nicer third, which probably included places such as Herts, Berks & Bucks so that it would be easy to pop into Town to do the shopping. As the sole judge he will, of course, pick Cordelia, hoping the des. res. would suitably impress the future son-in-law.

Goneril and Regan, like most daughters, know what will please their father and trot out the expected panegyric of undying affection and loyalty. At this point Lear turns, no doubt with a self-satisfied smile, to Cordelia. But now the confusion starts. Instead of rearranging the rehearsed platitudes of her sisters, Cordelia refuses to play, on the not unreasonable grounds that, as she is about to marry, she will have certain equal emotional and moral commitments to her future husband. Lear's response is to banish Cordelia and, for good measure, his faithful Earl of Kent who had the temerity to suggest that the king might have been a touch overhasty. Thus, leaving himself with no alternative but to divide his kingdom between Goneril and Regan.

Fortunately, the King of France sees more in Cordelia than a piece of real estate and is willing to marry her in any event. Kent is not so lucky. He is given six days to pack his bags and ten to leave the country on pain of death. With these two gone, there is no opposition to the elder daughters' plan to nip in the bud the 'unruly waywardness that infirm and choleric years bring' and bundle the old fool off to the appropriate Rest Home for Mothballed Monarchs. In fact Lear, on discovering that they will not let him have the trappings of kingship without the responsibilities, saves them the trouble by throwing what remain of the teddies out of the royal pram and, in a fit of maddened pique, storming out to set up home in a hovel on the blasted heath.

So are all the guys in the white hats out of the game? Who is to check the wicked sisters? The traditional contenders would have been the King of France, the Earl of Gloucester and his eldest son, Edgar. As the first has no need to meddle in the internal politics of Britain (even if he understood them) and Gloucester is hamstrung by the age-old dilemma as to whether he should serve his old king or his new masters, it seems that the mantle must fall on Edgar's shoulders. But the Gloucester family is a complicated state of affairs. Gloucester has another son, Edmund, who is illegitimate and realises that when the family solicitor calls the interested parties around the table to discuss the contents of the last will and testament, there will be nothing there for him. His only hope of arranging a redistribution of wealth in his direction is to discredit brother Edgar and take his place in the old man's affections. This he does, with apparent reluctance, by explaining to Gloucester that Edgar has tried to persuade him to join in a plot to kill their father and divide the money between them. At the same time he persuades Edgar that Cornwall is about to arrive to seize him as a traitor and the only option is to flee until the truth can be proved. Edgar complies, unwittingly confirming his father's suspicions. So Edmund, with a self-inflicted wound to show his loyalty, appears to be the only son to be trusted.

This leaves all the power firmly in the hands of Goneril and Regan, their husbands, who are bad or puny, and Edmund. The latter denounces his father as a confederate in a plot to overthrow the current regime. Cornwall believes the evidence, pronounces Gloucester a condemned traitor and rewards the loyal

Edmund with his father's earldom. There seems to be no one left to champion the cause of the moral good. Even the Fool appears by this time to have done a runner. Cue, in various guises and disguises, the Common Man!

First from the wings is a genuine common man, Cornwall's servant. He is forced to witness Gloucester's grotesque punishment for the so-called treachery and feels he has to intervene. The audience would see this as an act of physical and moral bravery. Not only is he certain to die but he also risks his mortal soul in this rebellion against his God-appointed Lord. Although he fails to save Gloucester's sight and his courage is rewarded by being stabbed in the back by Regan, there are some significant long-term effects. Having struck the first blow for natural justice, he has set a new moral tone and his fellow servants feel the need to tend to Gloucester's suffering rather than play safe and pass by on the other side. Their act of selflessness is confirmed by a former tenant of Gloucester who, disregarding his own safety, helps his ex-landlord escape from the terror and leads him, albeit inadvertently, into the care of his elder son. Finally, the Doctor shows similar compassionate consideration when tending to the mad Lear. None of these has anything to gain and clearly much to lose.

A second result of the servant's intervention is that in the ensuing scuffle he mortally wounds Cornwall. At first this seems little more than poetic justice but the ramifications cascade through the remainder of the play. Her husband's death leaves Regan a free agent to seize Edmund and, with his help, the kingdom. However, Goneril has similar designs and is already planning for Edmund to dispose of Albany while she poisons her sister. So worried is she that Regan will get her claws into Edmund, she sends her servant Oswald with a letter informing him of her plan.

En route, Oswald meets Gloucester, accompanied by Edgar, disguised as peasant. With an eye on a reward, Oswald attempts to capture Gloucester. Edgar intervenes and delivers a fatal blow. Oswald's dying wish is for his mistress's letter to be delivered. This act of feudal fidelity allows the plot to be revealed: Albany is made aware of the truth, Edgar is given the opportunity to challenge and slay Edmund in single combat and, having poisoned her sister, Goneril, realising that the game is up, commits suicide. Although this appears rather convoluted in description, it happens apace on stage and the audience is left to consider the relative merits of the actions of the two servants who put these matters in train.

We now come to the possible Common Men in disguise. Kent, Edgar and Lear have all lost their inherited powers and for a variety of reasons are forced to face life from the viewpoint of the ordinary man. As we have seen, Kent has been banished but, instead of sulking over the inequity, he decides to continue to serve Lear. The simple answer would have been to accompany Cordelia to the Court of France and at his leisure decide upon the best course of action. Instead, disguised, he enters into Lear's service as part of his retinue and by remaining in Britain hopes to help the king and broker a plan to bring the power of France to arrest the forces of evil. On the surface, this seems a selfless act on a par with that of Cornwall's servant or Gloucester's tenant. However, closer examination shows differences. Cornwall's servant is a servant while Kent is merely playing at one. The faithful tenant hopes for no reward. Kent hopes his sacrifice will earn the thanks of his king and the undying gratitude of Cordelia, which all sounds rather familiar.

He is successful to the extent that his invasion plans are the catalyst that brings about the downfall of Lear's tormentors, but this success is at the expense of Cordelia's life and earns little more than a nod of recognition from Lear. In fact, he has no higher ideal than Edmund. Each wishes to turn the situation to his own advantage. Kent is quite happy to restore the previous status quo without questioning its possible flaws. But what he feels at the end of the play is difficult to say. He seems more bemused than enlightened and, as a man unable to accept that a lifetime's conviction might be wrong, he throws in the towel.

Edgar, though, is younger and his experience of adopting the enforced disguise as the mad Bedlam beggar is much more illuminating. He realises that it is better to be openly despised than flattered and secretly despised. He sees the danger of concealing truth for whatever reason, as such deceit allows greater dangers to grow. Lear and Gloucester, by ignoring certain truths, opened the door to greater evils and their reaction to this is not to blame their own folly but to sink into a state of powerless vengeance or negative despair. Instead of demanding retribution, Edgar tends to his mutilated father and strives to save him from his belief that there is no point in life. In addition to his part in cleansing evil, he also brings to the fore the forces of mercy and compassion that are so necessary to save the play from being an exercise in nihilism.

Whereas Edgar and Kent take on their ignoble roles for a reason and to a greater and lesser extent learn from them, Lear is a confused mixture of the two. By stripping himself of his regal trappings and wandering naked in the storm of his mind, he sees, for the first time, life from the perspective of the ordinary person. As Gloucester only sees when he is blind, so Lear only comprehends when he is mad. However, the glimpses of truth–'The great image of Authority/A dog's obeyed in office', 'Plate sin with gold/And the strong lance of justice hurtless breaks', 'like a scurvy politician, seem/To see the things thou doest not'–are but gaps in the clouds of continued self-indulgence ranging from petulant rage to self-deceiving nostalgia. He serves to teach others but does not learn himself.

Although the play ends with the destruction of evil, there is no note of the triumphalism we hear at the end of *Macbeth*. The military victory, the usual symbol of success, lies not with Cordelia and France but with the astute Edmund. Cordelia, who seems to represent all that is worthy, is gratuitously murdered, Gloucester dies from exhaustion, Kent's efforts are scarcely acknowledged by the master he has tried so faithfully to serve and Lear dies in the foolish belief that Cordelia is still alive. And the curtain falls with Albany and Edgar playing pass the parcel with the crown of Britain.

If the message is not Henry IV's 'Thus ever did rebellion find rebuke', what is the audience to think? The play clearly casts doubts on the efficacy of a social structure based on authority and implicit obedience. It appears that those with power wish to indulge it or, at best, test its strength to ensure it still exists. There is a constant fear of an act of rebellion which can easily become a self-fulfilling prophecy. The circle is simple. Master beats servant to see if he still obeys him. Servant understandably reacts. Master, his worst suspicions having been vindicated, gives the servant the good thrashing he deserves. To ensure this upper hand, he must employ those who are willing to do his dirty work and that means open house to exploiters who will invent the laws, bullies who will enforce them and hypocrites who curry favour and power by dressing up self-interest as some inalienable truth.

If monarchy and its offspring are to be eschewed, what is the alternative? The play seems to suggest anarchy, an absence of law, not in the normally accepted sense of lawlessness, but in the sense of allowing natural justice to prevail, the sense of fairness that is tempered by compassion and founded on mental honesty. Certainly, when stripped of their furred robes, the former power-holders have doubts about the virtue of office. Whether Shakespeare had this in mind or not, history shows that if the abuse of authority is not held in check, then all the King's men, with or without horses, may never put Humpty together again.

# Wrapt In A Player's Hide

So far, the only voices in the plays to comment on the way things are run have come from the easily ignored sections of society–fools, women *et al.* This alternative comment can be dismissed by those who wish to do so as either inconsequential or dangerously subversive, according to mood. It therefore took not only artistic courage but also a certain amount of lateral thinking to make a dissentient the central tragic character and turn the malcontent into (in Goethe's opinion) 'a lovely, pure, noble and most moral nature'. But with Hamlet in *Hamlet*, Shakespeare apparently set out precisely to do that.

Hamlet has two problems, the general and the particular. The former is that he has to live in, as he sees it, a pointless world riven by hypocrisy and political intrigue. The latter, and later, is the imperative to avenge his father's death. For reasons that he fails fully to understand, he wishes to avoid both.

The first and ongoing difficulty could be avoided by escaping from Denmark. This is not as easy as it sounds, as both his mother and stepfather are set against it. So, in circumstances replicated in a longish line of mid-twentieth century rebels, with or without a cause, he reacts in a typically adolescent manner, i.e. indulging in private jokes and playing the martyr in a manner that is guaranteed to give maximum offence. If he hoped that the elder generation would eventually lose patience and pack the perpetual student back to Uni, his hopes were thwarted. The Ghost appears and this local difficulty cuts short his histrionics and brings him face to face with his worst fears and the realisation that not only was the time 'out of joint' but that he 'was born to set it right'.

So, what glue had shrunk in the woodwork? To the average observer, matters in Denmark appear to be well in hand. After the unfortunate death of Hamlet the Elder, Claudius and Gertrude have prevented potential internal squabbles through a swift and apparently happy alliance. The Norwegian threat has been averted through shrewd diplomacy and the tickish Fortinbras deployed at the expense of the Polacks. And, in the event of anything unforeseen going wrong, military preparations are well under way. Yet what is Hamlet so upset about? His mother's over-hasty marriage no doubt rankled but scarcely to the extent of inducing suicide. The emotional dilemma clearly runs deeper than that and his first soliloquy hints as much. Whatever the problem is, there seems no doubt that his solution is to avoid it by creating a play in which he is the lead, director and chief curtain-caller. After the prelude of his not-so-dumb show, he sets out on a more ambitious theatrical prevarication. Its substance is a play extempore: Hamlet strikes a pose, awaits a response, then develops the action. But the form, like most plays of the time, is in five acts.

Act One–the adoption of the antic disposition. By startling Ophelia with his red herring performance as the mad, rejected lover, he encourages Polonius to discover the 'truth'. This has the satisfying effect of arousing the suspicions of Claudius, upsetting his mother and inflaming Polonius with the thought of his own sagacity.

Act Two–the development of the antic disposition into the role of the Fool. The solution is to act rather than take action. He plays the Fool in such a manner that it puts Hamlet in control and justifies his procrastination. The appearance of Rosencrantz and Guildenstern, together with the strolling players, furthers this ambition. Now that the others are acting, Hamlet can get into his stride. He can play the Fool with impunity, knowing that they will have to play along with him. So, in due course, Polonius has to enter into a nebulous discussion on the shape of clouds and Rosencrantz and Guildenstern on the porosity of sponges, all equally helpless but to follow the script assigned them. If *en route* his behaviour puts obstacles between his duty and its accomplishment, then so much the better.

Act Three–the confrontation with Ophelia. This extraordinary outburst is at the heart of Hamlet's private drama. The possible motives are:

*(a)* he has genuine feelings of love for Ophelia and wants to save her from the rottenness of a world that in his view will inevitably corrupt her;

*(b)* he suspects she may be a plant and he wants to make it clear that he's not being gulled (the spin-off being that if Claudius or his spies are listening, the possibility of revenge will be further impeded);

*(c)* he is still disgusted with his mother's behaviour

and happily confuses her moral frailty and Ophelia's defencelessness to justify his misogyny;

*(d)* he is in such a bad temper with his own inadequacies that he is lashing out at the first thing he sees–the kick-the-cat syndrome.

In many ways this combination of compassion, hubris, bewilderment and self-disgust is at the core of his character and the scene as a whole, a dramatised version of the internal agonising suggested by his soliloquies.

Act Four–*The Mousetrap.* Hamlet, though suffering from first night nerves, is delighted that the introduction of the players will lead to his own *coup de théâtre.* The entertainment will be watched by the King and Queen unaware of Hamlet's interpolation, thus making it *a* play within *his* play within *their* play. Hamlet, hero of his own drama, is watching the real-life play of Claudius and Gertrude being confronted by their immoral actions, innocently performed by travelling players. As his confidence grows, he entwines the floor show with his practised role of Fool and Malcontent playing to his own gallery, embarrassing Ophelia as he wished to embarrass his mother. But, as he says, the play's the thing and if, in the basket of ulterior motives, he happens to catch the conscience of a king...

Act Five–his grand guignol. Having upset everyone whom he could possibly upset, he knows that if he continues to behave sufficiently outrageously even his mother will have him marked down as a dangerous lunatic and consent to his being shipped off to some bourn (in this case England) from which no traveller returns. There, after blagging his way through customs, he can take in a couple of shows and retire to a nunnery (aka Oxford) to write his treatise on *Mea Via Feci*. This variant on his original strategy is effected by frightening his mother to death, murdering the first intruder on his privacy and finally playing Hunt the Thimble with the body.

But what Hamlet had not taken into account when congratulating himself on the success of his theatrical productions was that behind him, watching Claudius and Gertrude watching the re-enactment of their crime, was not only the audience, intrigued as to the eventual outcome, but also someone or something else who knew exactly how everything would end up. Because Hamlet has dominated the stage to such an extent, it comes almost as much of a surprise to us as it does to him when it is discovered that he is by no means the master of his own destiny. Up to this moment he feels in complete control. He has dealt easily enough with the minor inconveniences of the snooping of Polonius and the spying of Rosencrantz and Guildenstern. He has also found a way of postponing the revenge by taking time to check on the Ghost's credentials. Even after *The Mousetrap* has confirmed Claudius' guilt, he can justify turning down the chance of killing the king at prayer on the grounds that it would do Claudius a favour if he died with his sins confessed. Once he had killed Polonius, he assumed that he would be kept under lock and key or, better still, sent abroad. Either way, he could no longer be held to account for his lack of action. If further catechised by the Ghost, he could at least claim that he had had a stab at it.

What he had not anticipated was the potential effect of his antics. His tormenting of Ophelia leads to her suicide and the man behind the curtain was not some out-of-town snoop whose death could be perceived as a hazard of the job but Polonius, chief Councillor of State. What is more, father to a son whose expression of filial duty to 'cut his [Hamlet's] throat i'th' church' ran along more traditional lines. Whether the deaths of his sister and father would have persuaded Laertes to hunt down Hamlet in the depths of Cowley is a matter for debate. The affair was resolved by a simple dramatic device–pirates.

Having discovered and altered his death warrant (so much for wanting to be dead), Hamlet must have felt that he was home and dry but he had no way of knowing that pirates–and how useful they and their ilk are to the beleaguered playwright–would intervene and send him back to Denmark. Once there, he quickly realises that he has lost control of the action. He is now in a drama written by another hand where he has been reduced to, if not a bit player, at least one now forced to react to rather than control the situation. No longer able to shape his destiny, he decides to change horses. In his new role, he casts himself as the innocent and tragic victim of circumstance, a man much put upon, who has been forced to spend his life dodging a cascade of earth-bound sparrows.

It is now Hamlet who seems a man of shreds and patches. His histrionic swan-song in and around Ophelia's grave is embarrassingly reminiscent of his previous castigation of the players who 'tear a passion to tatters, to very rags, to split the ears of the groundlings'. Our previous view of him as the self-assured puppetmaster is undermined when we realise he is easily outmanoeuvred by the machinations of Claudius and Laertes. Even the eventual killing of the king smacks more of petulance at being outwitted than a desire to adminster even-handed justice. Here is a man who previously held court with his quips and quiddities but now is outsmarted by no more significant a person than the Gravedigger Clown.

Whilst, in the emotionally charged atmosphere of the final scene, it is easy enough to accept Horatio's epitaph, 'Now cracks a noble heart', as an accurate reflection of Hamlet's worth, the truth must differ. If Horatio is to report Hamlet and his cause aright, the record would have to include the facts that, directly or indirectly, the sum of the Prince of Denmark's antics is: one suicide (intentional), one suicide (unintentional), three killings (unjustified), two killings (justifiable) and, in conclusion, the handing over of a kingdom so much enhanced by the valour of his father and the diplomatic skills of his uncle to, of all people, Norway.

So, how does all this square with Goethe's paean? Not obviously, but the playwright's skill is such that he has created more to Hamlet than his public face and when he is on stage alone we see aspects that Horatio, by definition, cannot report. It is these private utterances that have cast Hamlet as the tormented soul. Of the four soliloquies, two reflect an existing inner turmoil and two a reaction to the behaviour of others who seem to do things so much better than he.

In the first, we not only understand the depth of Hamlet's anger at the perceived insult to his father on the occasion of his mother's hasty and incestuous marriage but also his feeling of a larger unease about the whole situation in which he finds himself. Why must he hold his tongue? Is there something he knows that we don't? Or is he playing the martyr? All we can be sure of is that there is a sense that he is carrying a burden that he is unwilling to share even with the audience.

In the second, he sees the Player's enacted grief as a condemnation of his own cowardly dithering yet, on reflection, realises that ranting like a drab will not solve his problem. Similarly, in the fourth, he berates himself in the face of the determination and single-mindedness shown by Fortinbras. Yet again, he sees that such endeavour may well lose more than it gains. In each of these three there is an emotional outburst checked by a rational reappraisal and at the end of each neither he nor we are closer to gleaning what afflicts him. Intellectually he has sized up the situation, emotionally he has not.

It is only in the third and most renowned soliloquy that we get a glimpse of what lies at the heart of his distress. From the start, the tone is rational rather than inflammable. If we assume that the debate is not about the merits of suicide–as that option has already been rejected as against God's canon–we can reasonably accept that it is about the obverse: 'Is life worth living?' But perhaps there is a more particular question than that. Hamlet might not have been considering his own case so much as the general condition. Perhaps the complement that follows the verb has been left out, as, for example: 'To be [true to yourself]–or not to be [true to yourself]'. To follow the expected conventions (in Hamlet's case, filial obligations, marriage, political responsibility and general toeing of the line) or strike out for what you really believe or want, despite the risk of failure and universal scorn, or worse. (Shakespeare's suggested Catholicism would be apposite here.) To live comfortably in a world that has been created for you or to live in a world of your own uncertain creation.

In Hamlet's case, the dilemma cannot be reconciled–inaction is intolerable, the only action available is pointless. At a different time and in a different place matters might be clearer but he cannot escape the prison which is Denmark; one feels that even the grass in Wittenberg may be no greener. In the right light, his position could pass as tragic–a man rendered impotent by the weight of conflicting demands. But he and Shakespeare did not let it come to that. Hamlet is brought to his knees not by some fatal flaw born of a desire that he is later to regret. We see not the ill-conceived ambition of Macbeth nor the extravagant love of Othello, rather a man who sidesteps his destiny by the simple expediency of avoiding reality. As he cannot act, he must play–play the Fool, play with words, play on others' feelings and, finally, play with swords. When bewildered and frustrated by overwhelming circumstance, Hamlet took to playing as other men take to drink.

## Through A Looking Glass Darkly

If, as has been argued, *The Tempest* is in part a play about colonialism, then Prospero is a recognisable type of incomer. A misfit in his own land, he is washed up on foreign soil, his box of tricks under one arm and his gene-bank under the other. With Miranda in tow, he takes over the land and, after deceiving the natives with a variety of promises and long words, subjugates them to his own purposes. In this way he is given a second chance to practise the art of leadership and control and, more importantly, learn the lessons from the mistakes that allowed his brother to usurp his title as the Duke of Milan.

In this case, the locals number two. They–Ariel and Caliban–represent two types of the Common Man. The former, in the line of Malvolio and Oswald, has the wit to see that service can bring its own rewards, whilst the latter feels inherently uneasy in the role of underdog and is prepared to rebel to get what he sees as his rights. As Shakespeare has decided that Ariel is to be a whingeing, if somewhat self-satisfied, time-server, it is better to concentrate on Caliban.

What light does he throw on the overall picture of the subordinate classes? Whereas previous plays have supported subjection on the grounds that God had given responsibility to the few to rule for the benefit of the many, this myth is now abandoned and the truth is revealed. Prospero is in charge because he has the power to make Caliban do whatever he demands. If justification is needed to support the concept of slavery, then it is that Caliban is *(a)* stupid, *(b)* a threat to society and, above all, *(c)* ungrateful.

What are these claims so beloved by the law and order brigade and so often paraded to justify its views?

First, he lacks sufficient intellectual sensitivity to be treated as a human being. The evidence for this seems to rest on a reluctance to respond as a model pupil to some rudimentary lessons of astronomy and an early attempt at Tefling. In fact Caliban shows a singular perception as to what Prospero and his daughter are up to. We have seen from Cordelia's reaction in *King Lear* that language can be the tool of the master and in this case the reason for instructing Caliban is so that he can understand and obey orders. No wonder he has learnt to curse. Caliban also realises that in the exchange of knowledge, where he gave the 'qualities o' the isle' for some esoteric bits and pieces, he has come off by far the worse. If further evidence of the reality is needed, we only have to look at the language he uses to allay the fears of Stephano and Trinculo when hearing their tune replayed by an invisible Ariel:

> 'Be not afeard; the isle is full of noises,
> Sounds of sweet airs, that give delight and hurt not.'

Sounds that would lull him back to sleep and show him in his dreams such marvels

> 'that, when I waked,
> I cried to dream again.'

Hardly the language of an insensitive brute.

Second, that he is a threat to society. This is based on the general premise that he doesn't willingly do as he's told, even to the point of plotting rebellion, and the particular one that he attempted to rape Miranda. Whatever he might say to the contrary, Prospero has to accept that he has usurped Caliban and illegally taken control of his island. Whether on the basis of inheritance or possession, Caliban has the legal and moral right to ownership and as such he has an equal right to try to overthrow the invader by any reasonable means. Indeed, for Prospero to deny this would undermine his own case for reinstatement as the Duke of Milan. The echoes of his lofty aggrieved tone concerning his usurpation are still ringing round the stage when he explains to Miranda that the reason why he hasn't disposed of Caliban is that they cannot do without him as they have no one else to do the chores.

With regard to the attempted rape of Miranda, Prospero cannot have it both ways. If, as he claims, Caliban is a brute, then the desire to procreate is instinctive and without malice. The 'O ho, O ho!' is not, as it is often portrayed, a cry of gleeful lust but, according to the explorers of the time, was a common native way of expressing gratitude. It is not that Prospero wishes to protect his daughter's honour for her sake, more that he wishes to safeguard it until the best opportunity arrives. It seems the norm is that you trade your daughter in for power or possessions. Clearly, Caliban had neither of these to offer as Prospero had already confiscated both. When he accepts Ferdinand as a suitable son-in-law he wants, as part of the arrangement, to ensure Miranda's virginity until the deal is signed, sealed and delivered. If Ferdinand were to change his mind–and indeed his father might persuade him to do so–then at least the commodity would be still marketable. It is more Prospero than Caliban who is trying to manipulate Miranda to his own advantage.

The third charge was that Caliban was ungrateful. This has always been a very subtle form of bullying or emotional blackmail and is always difficult to refute, particularly when you are the recipient of gifts that are given more for the benefit of the donor than the donee. It smacks of the more-in-sorrow-than-in-anger interview over the end of term report. *After all the sacrifices that your mother and I have made*, etc, etc. I mean, the poor lad didn't ask to be sent to an advantaged educational establishment. In truth, if anyone should be grateful, it is Prospero for being shown how to distinguish between 'the fresh springs', 'brine-pits', 'barren places and fertile'. The gifts of knowledge and language made in return are, as we have seen, double edged. This truth is further underlined if we summarise Prospero's discourse with Ariel on the subject:

| | |
|---|---|
| *Prospero:* | Did I free you from the tree-trunk? |
| *Ariel:* | Yes. |
| *Prospero:* | Are you grateful? Will you do as I say? |
| *Ariel:* | Yes. Yes. |
| *Prospero:* | If not, I'll put you back in the tree. |
| *Ariel:* | There's no answer to that. |

In Prospero's eyes, the presence of gratitude is the outward sign of obedience and the absence the mark of the rebel. As Macbeth *et al.* demonstrate, it is the uncertainty that the king feels about his right to rule, rather than doubts concerning his ability to do so, that makes for acts of tyranny.

Although the eventual consequence of colonialism is seen only indistinctly in the mirror of *The Tempest*, the vision is developed in later literary works, in particular Conrad's *Heart of Darkness*, and finally exploded in various reactions to the Vietnam war, notably Coppola's *Apocalypse Now.* Although Coppola's firework display has much to say on the true nature of war as it relates to colonial ambition, it is the imagery of Conrad that is closer to Shakespeare. This acts as an excuse to compare the ideas present in the play with those more fully expressed some three hundred years later.

Like Shakespeare, Conrad felt that the pressures of the time required him to veil his criticism of his intended target–the exploitation of Africa by the Europeans under the guise of improving the lot of the natives. He employs a narrator, Charlie Marlow, who describes, without much in the way of overt comment, the events that he witnesses. Marlow, a common sailor with a known propensity for spinning yarns, was the ideal riddle through which the author could filter his opinions. As with other Common Men, it is easy enough, if you wish, to dismiss what Marlow has to say as the disaffection of someone who does not have the appropriate overview to make a real judgement. Yet the author can hope that a sense of uneasiness in the reader is likely to linger.

Marlow, out of work, has to use the influence of his aunt to find a job. This good lady has the ear of those who wish to save the natives from their heathen practices and persuades the relevant authority that her nephew would be just the man to take command of a river steamer on the Congo. It turns out that the purpose of the voyage is to search for Kurtz, a much revered, if eccentric, agent of the company who has gone AWOL. In fact, rather than follow the mission statement to save the heathen souls and as much ivory as possible, Kurtz–like Prospero–has with his superior fire-power enlisted the help of the locals to set up his own fiefdom. This is the keystone of a grand design to control the whole of the continent which he would in due course hand over to a suitably grateful nation.

As the steamer had been wrecked and Marlow had to travel overland to carry out the necessary repairs, he has much time on his hands to observe the consequence of colonisation on those it most directly affected. It was soon apparent that, whatever sentiments might be expressed in his aunt's circle as to the worthiness of the enterprise, the truth was it had 'no more moral purpose at the back of it than there is in burglars breaking into a safe.'

The treatment of the natives is not dissimilar to

Prospero's treatment of his subjects. Some were reduced from a state of 'wild vitality, an intense energy of movement that was as natural and true as the surf along their coast' to a condition of sub-human indifference 'lying confusedly in the greenish gloom' and,

> 'Brought from all the recesses of the coast in all the legality of time contracts, lost in uncongenial surroundings, fed on unfamiliar food, they sickened, became inefficient and were then allowed to crawl away and rest.' (cf. Stephano's and Trinculo's plans for a dead Indian.)

Others, like Ariel, had joined with the oppressor and were rewarded with NCO status. Marlow came across such a one in charge of the 'criminals' who had failed to fulfil their contractual responsibilities. He was

> 'one of the reclaimed, the product of the new forces at work ... carrying a rifle by its middle. He had a uniform jacket with one button off, and seeing a white man on the path, hoisted his weapon to his shoulder with alacrity. This was simple prudence,

white men being so much alike at a distance that he could not tell who I might be. He was speedily reassured, and with a large, white, rascally grin, and a glance at his charge, seemed to take me into partnership in his exalted trust. After all, I also was a part of the great cause of these high and just proceedings.'

There are many telling examples of how the interlopers bulldozed their way through another culture, but two will suffice. The first has its echoes of that Prospero wannabe, Stephano:

> 'Once a white man in an unbuttoned uniform, camping on the path with an armed escort of lank Zanzibaris, very hospitable and festive–not to say drunk. Was looking after the upkeep of the road, he declared. Can't say I saw any road or any upkeep, unless the body of a middle-aged negro, with a bullet in his forehead ... may be considered as a permanent improvement.'

and the second, when a grass shed containing various trash to trade for ivory burst into flames, shows the inevitable outcome when those in charge can never admit to being at fault:

> 'The shed was already a heap of embers glowing fiercely. A nigger was being beaten nearby. They said he had caused the fire in some way; be that as it may, he was screaming most horribly. I saw him, later, for several days, sitting in a bit of shade looking very sick and trying to recover himself: afterwards he arose and went out–and the wilderness without a sound took him into its bosom again.'

This only supported the view held by the Europeans that the natives, far from grasping the unique opportunity that was to improve their existence, behaved in a shiftless and irresponsible manner, taking the first opportunity to clear off and leave their benefactors in the lurch. But as Marlow points out:

> 'Well, if a lot of mysterious niggers armed with all kinds of fearful weapons suddenly took to travelling on the road between Deal and Gravesend, catching the yokels right and left to carry heavy

loads for them, I fancy every farm and cottage thereabouts would get empty very soon.'

But enough are enlisted to complete the journey and eventually Marlow finds the dying Kurtz, along with the report that he had been entrusted to compose for the International Society for the Suppression of Savage Customs. This begins with the statement that we whites

> 'must necessarily appear to them [savages] in the nature of supernatural beings–we approach them with the might as of a deity, *and so on and so on.* By the simple exercise of our will we can exert a power for good practically unbounded,' etc, etc.

Marlow, though impressed by the language, cryptically remarks that there was little in the way of exposition of method to put these uplifting aims into operation. That is, unless it was the scrawled post scriptum apparently added at some later date:

> 'Exterminate all the brutes!'

An ultimate solution that, if circumstance demanded, would receive the nod from Prospero, Henry V and, in due course, a certain would-be painter from Austria.

# Ill-Considered Coastlines & Other Trifles

With *The Winter's Tale,* Shakespeare seems to have found a vehicle to redress certain imbalances. Order is restored, not through the usual general mayhem; the good succeed, without the accompanying triumphalism. Girl power at last comes to the fore and the honest yeoman upstages the unscrupulous rogue who does good against his will.

The play opens with the not unfamiliar scene of the man who holds the cards exercising his feudal rights to do whatever he wants. Leontes, King of Sicilia, in a whim of self-indulgence tries to persuade his lifelong friend Polixenes, King of Bohemia, to extend his visit. Polixenes refuses on the grounds that he ought reasonably to be seeing to the affairs of his realm. Leontes sets Hermione, his wife, on to his fellow king to persuade him to stay beyond his allotted time. When she, no doubt with courtesy and charm, succeeds, Leontes convinces himself that she has been

Polixenes' lover and that the child she is carrying is his bastard. This combination of Lear and Othello might have had even those two exponents of unstable behaviour shaking their heads. At least the former could plead impending senile insanity and the latter that he was gulled by Iago, whereas Leontes had no such excuse. Indeed, all and sundry combined to protest Hermione's innocence.

Despite this, Leontes powers his way into proving what he wants to believe by the simple trick of condemning to death those he believes guilty. He does this by persuading Lord A (Camillo) to get rid of Polixenes by feeding him a 'ling'ring dram' that won't kick in until he is safely out of the country and Lord B (Antigonus) to dispose of the bastard child by dumping her in 'some remote and desert place'. Camillo, unlike the pusillanimous Gaunt, is willing to discriminate between proper behaviour and feudal loyalty. Using his authority to unlock the city's gates and telling Polixenes of his lifelong friend's intentions, they both escape to Bohemia. Antigonus is less scrupulous and takes Perdita, as she will be called (oops, given away the ending), to Bohemia. He gives her what Leontes has decided is the perfectly reasonable chance of either being rescued by a strolling shepherd or eaten by a passing carnivore. There is, therefore, a certain sense of *schadenfreude* when Antigonus is caught by a Bohemian bear and devoured alive.

Meanwhile, back at the hacienda, Leontes is trying to substantiate his actions by giving Hermione a fair trial:

> 'Let us be cleared
> Of being tyrannous, since we so openly
> Proceed in justice'
> (Pinochet, eat your heart out.)

He has sent to the Oracle in Delphi who has replied in surprisingly unequivocal terms that Hermione is innocent, Polixenes is innocent and Leontes is beyond the pale.

True to form, Leontes immediately dismisses the agreed scheme of arbitration as mere falsehood and insists that the trial of Hermione should continue–counts against her now having been raised from adultery to conspiracy, treason and attempted regicide. No sooner have the proceedings restarted than he learns, first, from a servant, that Mamillius, his only son and heir, has died in 'mere conceit and fear' because of the treatment being handed out to his mother and, seconds later, from Paulina, wife to Antigonus and champion of the Queen's cause, that Hermione has also fatally collapsed under the pressure. Leontes, as the latest member of a long line of not too clever tragic heroes, realises that he has made a dreadful mistake. However, there are still two acts (and, as it turns out, sixteen years) to go so, whatever your feelings about the justice of the situation, it seems inevitable that things may turn out for the better and that Leontes will not have to play the Roman fool.

Even before this, the audience knows that the lost Perdita has been found, together with certain items that might be used in the identifying process in due course. However, the devouring bear and the sinking of the ship with all hands have removed all contemporary witness and, although the Shepherd who found and adopted her suspected that she might be more than she seemed, at the end of Act III there was no clear sign how matters would resolve themselves.

In fact, what Shakespeare does is re-wind the story

whilst fast-forwarding the action. Florizel, son of Polixenes, comes across the now marriageable Perdita whilst out hunting, falls in love with her and spends more time than usual away from home. Polixenes is informed that he is hanging about the skirts of some peasant girl and fears the worst. With the help of Camillo, he tracks them down to a Sheep Shearing celebration where Perdita has been chosen to be the Mistress of the Feast. Having confirmed the truth and informed the various parties that Florizel would be disinherited, the Shepherd hanged or worse and Perdita facially disfigured if the two ever met again, he departs, confident that that is the end of that particular piece of nonsense. However Florizel, like Hermione, is made of sterner stuff. With the help of Camillo, the couple, disguised, plan to escape to Sicilia where, with letters of introduction, they can present themselves to the court of Leontes as envoys from Polixenes, enjoined to rebuild fences. The Shepherd and his son, no doubt fearing a regal change of mind, are all too ready to join the venture and also land in Sicilia.

At this point Shakespeare has to unleash a posse of Gents to keep the audience up to date with the off-stage activities which it needs to know for the purposes of the denouement:

*(a)* Polixenes in fury has arrived in Sicilia.

*(b)* Polixenes has bumped into Shepherd and Son.

*(c)* The Shepherd has offered evidence of identity that Perdita is not really his daughter and so he's not really to blame.

*(d)* Several witnesses have jumped out of the woodwork to confirm authenticity of relics and the real identity of Perdita,

so that

*(e)* Leontes realises that Perdita is his lost daughter.

*(f)* The oracle can be proved right.

*(g)* Polixenes can preen himself that the lad couldn't have done better if he'd tried.

*(h)* Polixenes and Leontes can congratulate themselves that the political situation has been most satisfactorily resolved.

If that were not enough, it turns out that Hermione is not dead but has been kept hidden by Paulina (apparently without complaint) all the time and is finally produced by a somewhat improbable *coup de théâtre* and returned to her grateful owner. Antigonus, now cleared of infanticide, is seen as the unwitting saviour. By proxy, Paulina is rewarded for her persistence and this takes the inevitable form of another husband in the shape of the faithful Camillo. As the curtain falls, you can almost hear Leontes begging Polixenes to extend his visit and asking for any volunteers to support his plea.

So where is the Common Man in all this? In the first half Paulina manfully tries to point out the errors of Leontes' ways but he who dismisses the Delphic Oracle is hardly likely to listen to a female Fool. Indeed, her protestations merely confirm his belief that women need to be curbed and that her husband is remiss in his duties. In the second, what with all the plot expositions and song-and-dance routines, there is little room for measured observation. However, there are a couple of matters worth looking at.

First, there is Autolycus, a rogue out to fleece the country bumpkins. Though successful in various acts of dishonesty, he is forced by circumstances to become the agent of good. He changes clothes with Florizel to help the lovers escape and in his new-found courtier's habit is able to persuade Shepherd father and son to join him on the boat to Sicilia, rather than selfishly spilling the beans to Polixenes. His motive is that he might be rewarded by his former master Florizel but happily it is those that he has gulled who eventually profit from his act. In his equivocation,

> 'if I thought it were a piece of honesty to acquaint the king withal, I would not do't: I hold it more knavery to conceal it; and therein am I constant to my profession.'

he seems reminscent of Falstaff, but he does not share Falstaff's capacity for self-deceit. He realises, like Feste and Lear's Fool, that dishonesty thrives not because of the cleverness of the rogue but rather through the vainglorious foolishness of others. In fact, he is almost a benign Iago. With the opportunity for playing to the gallery and incisive sardonic comment, he seems a mixture of the parts played by Armin and Kemp. Perhaps in this creation Shakespeare laid one particular ghost to rest. However preposterous the final scene between rogue and clown, it still contains that element of human decency and good humour that is so lacking in the behaviour of their betters.

The second is the admirable moral stance taken by Perdita. Although in love with Florizel, she is not so bowled over that she does not see the potential disaster inherent in their courtship. She also realises that being 'goddess-like prank'd up' as Mistress of the Feast does not mean that she is any way better than she was before, a lesson that took Lear eighty years and a bout of lunacy to comprehend. We see this at best when she welcomes the disguised Polixenes with a gift of flowers. He dismisses the gift of rosemary and rue as dismal flowers of winter and recommends that she should cultivate 'carnations and streak'd gillyvors', flowers that are created by marrying a gentle scion to a baser stock. Given that he is trying to prevent the relationship between a prince and a shepherdess, this might appear ironic. But in Polixenes' eyes there was probably nothing wrong with a bit of noble grafting on the side. It was marriage beneath one's station that was morally and politically reprehensible. However, Perdita sticks to her side of the GM argument with steady dignity and a clarity of thought that more than favourably contrasts with the febrile judgements of the so-called heads of state.

Where does all this leave us? Those that support the play see it as a masque to celebrate a royal wedding, a symbolic re-enaction of the greatest of human virtues, forgiveness and reconciliation, but surely even they must ask a question or two. Why, if only as a political expedient, did Leontes *(Surely you can see that it wasn't completely my fault?)* not remarry to secure an heir? Why did Polixenes take his attempted murder on the chin and not plot revenge? Pour poison in Leontes' ear and marry Hermione, perhaps? Why did Hermione accept being locked away for sixteen years when she must have known that Leontes had accepted her innocence? If she didn't know, why hadn't Paulina told her? And what on earth happened to Perdita? Once she is involved in the male machinations of the flight to Sicilia she has only one thing to say,

> 'I see the play so lies
> That I must bear a part.'

and the part is–do what you're told and, if in doubt, kneel. What happened to that plucky young girl who said her piece to the Headmaster to the silent admiration of the Lower Sixth? Jonson completely missed the point when criticising Shakespeare's grasp of geography. Of course Bohemia had a coast line and it probably also had a dog called Nana. In the end the reality was never intended to be there but in another world, where those with power can simply say *I'm sorry* when they commit any variety of atrocity and, by that mutually agreed shibboleth, wipe the slate clean.

## But There Again

So, if *The Winter's Tale* is something approaching Shakespeare's final word, we are back to the question: where does that leave us? Are we to assume that there has been a change of attitude? In the profitable world of courtly masques, has he succumbed to the piper-payers and has he, as Hamlet so carefully guarded against, become the instrument that can be played to their tune? Is the rustle we hear in the background the sound of future Headmasters rubbing their hands?

At first sight it seems that there is a case. In previous plays, for example *Macbeth* and *King Lear*, Shakespeare has cast serious doubts on the inalienable right to exercise power in order to achieve a desired effect. The possession of power means the fear of losing power and the fear of losing it leads to using it to test the water, usually with disastrous effect. So Lear and Macbeth, who either failed to foresee or chose to ignore the result of the abuse or misuse of power, are similarly and aptly punished by destroying the order they claim to uphold and by losing the very things they were striving to gain and protect, respectively a favourite daughter and feudal loyalty. Even when the dust has settled, the audience is left with the feeling that the return to order is at best tenuous and at worst cosmetic. A point effectively illustrated in Polanski's version of *Macbeth* when the film concludes with Malcolm's brother Donalbain galloping off in search of the witches' coven to see what might be in store for him.

However, in *The Winter's Tale*, Leontes attempts to smash everything that he can get his hands on, yet seems to get off scot free, apart from the death of Mamillius. Even that is offset by the acquisition of the ideal son-in-law.

Do we, therefore, conclude that the one-time scourge of political bullies has been reduced to reworking musical comedies? This might be true if Shakespeare's main and apparent purpose was political satire. If we were talking about a George Orwell who, in his later years, had penned *Animal Farm Regained,* where the pigs, repentant, embrace the Marxist teachings of Old Major and the chickens and sheep live happily ever after, we could reasonably assume that he had sold out to the enemy or lost his marbles or both. But Orwell's way was never Shakespeare's way. And at the heart of Shakespeare's lay equivocation where nothing is as it immediately seems.

Even a cursory reading of his plays reveals the writer's interest in the idea of appearance and reality and the interconnection between theatre and life. A world where the opposite of a truth is not necessarily a lie. The somewhat acrimonious scene between Henry and his soldiers on the night before the battle of Agincourt depends entirely on this idea for its dramatic tension. To the audience, the disguised king is still the king who could imperiously sweep aside any objections. But if he is to conceal his plan he cannot be the king. He must adopt another course of action to achieve his ends. Shakespeare was quick to realise the variety of theatrical advantages that this offered. It might help to look at one or two examples.

Disguise again. Not only did it allow dramatic irony but, in the case of Viola in *Twelfth Night,* it offered character insight. Disguised, for her own protection, as a young man, she falls in love with Orsino. He employs her as a go-between to woo Olivia and counts on her as a good chap to further his cause. Her dual role allows the audience to experience the to-and-fro of the character acting the part of a man but living the part of a woman, which in turn shows her emotions torn between doing what she ought and saying what she feels. Although this lends itself to comedy with challenges to sword fights and manly slaps on the back, it will return in a more dreadful manner in *King Lear*. Here Edgar and Gloucester, the disguised madman and his eyeless father, enact a scene where the full implication is known only to the audience who can interpret the sentiments of one character through the experiences of the other.

Shakespeare deals with ideas and themes in a similar manner. The all-seeing Fool shows the truth to the unseeing Lear. Yet the truth is powerless before the empowered stupidity. This dichotomy is at the centre of the tragedy. On another occasion, he places Henry V on one side of the moral see-saw and Pistol (or, more improbably, Falstaff) on the other. The king is clearly the hero and Pistol the villain. But as the play progresses and the balance begins to settle, matters do not seem quite so clear cut. We begin to realise that the question is not whether the heroics of

Henry or the cowardice of Pistol will settle the outcome of the battle (after all, that was a given) but whether either should be there at all, or in the Falklands, or Vietnam, or anywhere else for that matter. Pistol may well be reprehensible but how much is he the product of his King's ambitions?

While we're on things being not exactly what they seem, we might return to Jonson and his fulminations over Shakespeare's careless disregard of cartographical niceties concerning the seaboard of Eastern Europe, and look at a couple of other inconsistencies. First, in *Henry V*, Shakespeare gets the king to order the slaughter of all the French prisoners (twice) and then resurrects them (or at least 1500 of them) a scene or so later. Second, the childless Lady Macbeth has apparently suckled a child, as she explains she is prepared to tear it from her breast and dash its brains out rather than break her word. No doubt logical explanations could be found for both–previous husbands or military orders distorted though transmission, etc–and in all probability these inconsistencies would be missed in a live production. However, it may well be wrong to regard them as a thoughtless oversight on the playwright's part.

Let's start with *Henry V.* Shakespeare needs the king to order the death of the French prisoners on two different occasions for two different reasons. First, to show Henry's incisive leadership (*we'll talk about the Geneva Convention later*) and second, his moral indignation at the blatant breach of the rules of war by the enemy. Then, at a later stage, the playwright needs them alive to supply the English Herald with numerical evidence to demonstrate the extent of the glorious victory.

These three moments are extremely important in establishing what is going on in Henry's or, for that matter, any war leader's mind. The key factors are success at all costs (Hiroshima), excusing revenge on the grounds of justice (retaliatory bombing of Hamburg and Dresden) and suitable statistics–one dead Davy Gam is worth 1500 quivering Frenchmen–to answer any post-war criticism *(Never have so many owed so much,* etc). By concentrating the audience's attention on the French prisoners, he can draw these ideas together with particular dramatic effect, so that in a moment they can see Henry as single-minded/wrathful/compassionate or ruthless/vindictive/scheming according to their viewpoint. As any student of political propaganda will tell you, whether the prisoners are actually alive or dead is completely irrelevant.

With Lady Macbeth, Shakespeare has a different problem. Regardless of the question of succession to the throne, it is dramatically important that she has no children. At least, in the sense that the only nursing and nurturing she has to do relates to her husband. The moral support that he will require to achieve his ambition cannot be side-tracked by nappies and Early Learning Centres. To achieve the ultimate goal there must be no distraction, no Fleance to confuse the issue. However, when her contribution is ignored, as it will be when Macbeth has sufficient confidence to think he can manage on his own,

> 'Be innocent of the knowledge, dearest chuck,
> Till thou applaud the deed'

and she collapses under the strain which she has mostly borne, we must feel pity and not delight at her fall. In order for the sleepwalking scene to work, we must have had a glimpse of a softer, more compassionate side to her character. To dash out her baby's brains is the most horrific thing she can think of to demonstrate her loyalty. A 'fiend-like Queen' would do it without compunction and scarcely think it worthy of the mention.

This is only the first in a series of hints, which include the need to build up Dutch courage before the murder, the resemblance of Duncan to her father, possibly the fainting after the murder, the attempt to comfort Macbeth when he realises the threat that Banquo might prove, and the remorse she shows over the death of Lady Macduff. All combine to create the desired effect. In fact, the image of the childless mother is at the centre of her tragedy.

The point of this digression from *The Winter's Tale* is to show that Shakespeare can easily be playing more than one game and that it is often the apparent inconsistencies and contradictions that give his plays their strength. So the proposition, *As it was right for Lear to be punished for his folly, so it is equally wrong for Leontes to escape punishment for his,* may not be as clear-cut as it appears. Are these plays in fact a variation on a theme? We can look at them in terms of either substance or form.

First the substance. The titles really give the whole

thing away. If they had been respectively *A Storm in a Teacup* and *King Leontes*, we might have had two very different plays. In the event, *King Lear* is, as it suggests, a play about one individual that examines the ebb and flow of events as it affects him. Whereas *The Winter's Tale* is less about the people as individuals and more about how they contribute to the moral pattern as a whole. In any fable you expect a certain amount of stereotyping and the help of outside agencies to move the story to its conclusion. There is nothing to be gained by showing Leontes bewailing his lot in the Sicilian wilderness, always assuming it had one. The questions the play asks are: *In general, can things turn out well?* and *What does that statement really mean?*

Second, the form or structure of the two plays. *King Lear* follows the well tried formula of folly followed by fall, first through Lear and then through Gloucester. *The Winter's Tale* is more complex. For a start, it has three parts or rather movements, as each is self-contained yet contributes to the whole. The first is extremely short, lasting less than one hundred lines and can be compared to the closing scene of *The Merchant of Venice.* Two close male friends, together with the wife of one of them, appear in a state of harmony. In the case of *The Merchant*, we know that this satisfactory arrangement might not have been so. The continuance of the friendship between Antonio and Bassanio had been threatened by the latter's need to marry a rich heiress (he clearly wasn't prepared to work for a living) and the former's foolish bond with Shylock. The Lady, however, far from being the threat is the saviour, providing cash with one hand and legal niceties with the other. Portia symbolically even hands over the letter that contains the news that Antonio's fortune is not lost after all. As the curtain drops, it seems all must be well for ever and a day.

So it must have seemed at the opening of *The Winter's Tale.* Polixenes is explaining to Hermione that since the days of pure youthful love shared between himself and Leontes, 'temptations have been born' in the shape of the opposite sex. They both had to get married for political reasons but fortunately the feared corruption had been averted, the friendship has prospered and both wives have produced male heirs. Lights dim to appropriate music. However, this is not to be. It is as though Bassanio suddenly starts wondering how it is that Portia should know so much about Antonio's commercial affairs and why he 'shall not know by what strange accident [Portia] chanced on this letter'. Indeed, why was she so keen to save Antonio in the first place?

The second movement is a partial reworking of *King Lear.* Leontes/Lear banishes the one person, Hermione/Cordelia, whom he has every reason to trust, loses his heir/kingdom only to realise his folly too late, while Polixenes/Gloucester decides to disinherit his son Florizel/Edgar, without being in possession of the full facts. Camillo/Kent flutters around trying to keep a finger in the dyke and Paulina/Fool tells the truth only to be ignored.

But it is the third and last movement that takes Shakespeare's dramatic experiment a step forward. Restoration and redemption occur not as a convenient afterthought but as a natural progression of what has gone before. During the play's blackest moments the forces of repair are constantly at work. Paulina and Camillo are much more purposeful than their counterparts in *King Lear.* They do not accept that because the 'great wheel' has fallen, all lesser mortals must fall too and they set about first salvaging, then restoring the situation. Improbable as some of the detail might be, their acts seem to have a greater chance of long-term success than that of throwing money at the problem, coupled with a clever piece of legal legerdemain. In the same period of time, Perdita is developing a set of values that Florizel will cherish for their own sake. Unlike his father, he is prepared to marry a woman for what she is, rather than as some sort of cloning exercise.

Back to the question. Can things turn out well and what exactly does 'well' mean? In its common dramatic sense, 'well' means that the feared result is avoided, usually against expectation, and in that sense *The Merchant of Venice* turns out well. The worst that could have happened would have been that Portia would have married against her wishes and Antonio would have died because of imprudent borrowing on behalf of his friend. Both are avoided. But it is the negativity of this sense of 'well' that is unsatisfactory. The final curtain leaves a number of loose ends. Will Jessica really be at ease in a gentile community that has spat upon her race? Having taken such a risk, will Antonio leave Bassanio and retire gracefully to Venice? Why, unlike Gratiano, does Bassanio show so little enthusiasm at the idea of consummating his marriage? Will Portia readily sacrifice her independence? In the end, the conclusion is as tenuous or as cosmetic as any of the political dramas.

In *The Winter's Tale*, Shakespeare examines the alternative interpretation: that is, the hoped-for result is achieved despite various attempts to thwart it. A case of *All's Well that Starts Well.* There is no doubt that the play fits this pattern rather than that of the overthrow of evil against the odds. The death of Mamillius illustrates the difference between this drama and the preceding tragedies. When the death is announced, the audience would assume that it was part of the just punishment that Leontes deserved and a further blow for Hermione to bear. But in fact it is the catalyst that allows the forces of goodness and order to return. Not only, now that she is childless, can Hermione reasonably take part in Paulina's plan but also the old order has been conveniently castrated. Leontes is at pains to show that Mamillius is a chip off the old block and there is no doubt how he would have brought him up. Without him, we feel at the end of the play that Sicilia will be in safer, wiser hands as the old men fade away, leaving a benign matriarchy to guide a younger generation who have seen the folly of patriarchal preconceptions.

If this gives the impression of a neat and tidy explanation, then that is equally wrong. For this is a winter's tale to be spun out over long evenings where the pictures in the coals are as important as the details of the plot and the nudged memories of the listeners as telling as the feelings of fictional kings and queens. The fire burns; the meaning flickers. And so it is with Shakespeare. Just when you think you've got him firmly grasped, he slips past the tackle. No matter how hard the Marxists, the Feminists, the Post-Neo-Reconstructionalists and the Headmasters of England try, he will not conform. Little is known of his life but one thing's for sure. He was never made Head Boy of the Grammar School in Stratford-upon-Avon.

# A List

As the nature of the Contents does its best to conceal which particular plays are under discussion, I thought it might be helpful to provide the reader with a list. However, since the book is as much about the characters as the plays, I felt it right and proper to have another list. Unfortunately, this left a group of personages, often renowned, who, clearly, might be upset if ignored altogether.

So the list, like the much put-upon Henry VI, has three parts: the plays, the participants and the public in general and particular. As with all lists, those with the inclination should feel free to tick off as appropriate.

## The Plays

# The Participants

## The Public



Authors of books who know what they are about have a rather different arrangement, which they call an Index.